THIS BOOK BELONGS TO:

_____

THIS BOOK IS A GIFT WITH BEST COMPLIMENTS

TO: _____

FROM: _____

VOICE
AND
WISDOM™

OUR JOURNEY TO ONENESS

RAMANJANEYULU TANGUTURI

Printed in the United States of America

ISBN 979-8-9988396-0-3

Library of Congress Control Number: 2025939174

Published with permission by Ekatva Publishing, LLC

Book cover art copyright Ekatva Publishing, LLC

www.onenessmission.world

Reprinted with Permission: Excerpts from the book by Neihardt, John G., Black Elk Speaks, (Lincoln, NE: Bison Books, 2014). Reprinted with permission from the John Neihardt Trust.

Reprinted with Permission: excerpts from the Denkard: Dk 6:31 and 6:b47(trans. Mills) and excerpts from the following: avesta.org/zfaq.html and avesta.org/yasna/indes.html#y35 Reprinted with permission of Joseph Peterson.

Reprinted with Permission: Enrico Cerulli. The folk-literature of the Galla of Southern Abyssinia. p. 137. Public domain. Reprinted with permission from Seltzer Books.

Reprinted with Permission: African Traditional Religions - Will Coleman, Ph.D. (Baba Esuyemi Ifayemi), Associate Professor at the Interdenominational Theological Center, Awo Fa'lokun Fatunmbi, with assistance from Brad Ost, Head of Reference Services and Theological Librarian at the Atlanta University Center Robert W. Woodruff Library https://research.auctr.edu/Ifa/Chap9Prayer

Reprinted with Permission: Appendix Photo of Teaching at a Yoga Teacher training course in the Dalles, Oregon, USA. Published with permission from Pure Yoga Teacher Training, the Dalles, Oregon.

Epistle to the Son of the Wolf, by Mírzá Ḥusayn-'Alí Núrí known as Bahá'u'lláh https://www.gutenberg.org/cache/epub/16697/pg16697-images.html Printed with permission from Bahai.org

CONTENTS

ACKNOWLEDGEMENTS

I wish to express GRATITUDE to God—the one whose existence I doubted (and even hated a few times)—for not giving up on me, for teaching me with patience and persistence in His amazing Voice and for leading me to write this book.

To my wife, Dawn Camille Knight Tanguturi, who, prompted by God, understood my flaws, revealed how God led her to marry me, showed me the Love of God, risked her life for me, challenged me, stood by me, enabled me to know the purpose of my life, walked with me and walked in obedience to God to publish this book and make it happen.

DEDICATION

This book is dedicated to the Voice and to the mission statement given to me:

To promote and bring peace and joy through oneness of humanity with the One God and worshipping in Oneness with love.

PREFACE

The Voice I heard was soothing yet strong, soft yet clear as a ringing bell, refreshing like a waterfall from the highest mountain, penetrating though not piercing, passing through every cell of my body at the same time, deep and filled with love, creating in me a longing to hear more and more. On and on I can go and yet fall short of words to describe it. Whenever I heard the Voice, it was an indescribable and unique experience; I enjoyed and cherished every moment every time. I was ten years old when I first heard the Voice. I am now nearing my eighty-first birthday.

Papa Ram
Ramanjaneyulu (Rom) Tanguturi
June 2023

VOICE

CHAPTER 1

THE VOICE

CONTEMPLATION, DREAM AND VISION

Every human being, regardless of lifestyle, status, unbelief or belief in God, religion, or faith, has a desire to live in peace and joy. But history shows there has been so much damage, destruction, war and shedding of blood through the misuse of religion and the name of God. Too many people want to impose their beliefs and practices on others, condemning those whose philosophies and customs are different from their own—some even going so far as to cause harm or loss of life. Depending on their status or level of resources, they may do this on a large scale, all for the purpose of enhancing self-centered power and control.

It has been my dream and vision from childhood to see the world in its glory with peace and joy, filled with love, free from bloodshed in the name of God or religion. I am not a scholar nor a theologian—not even a voracious reader!—just a common man habituated to listening, learning and setting aside the contradictions, controversies and condemnations in what others say. My quest for this dream has only gotten stronger and stronger over the years. Many times, seeing how religion was used destructively, I doubted whether there was a God at all.

I decided to engage with as many scholars and theologians of different faiths as possible, utilizing every occasion and opportunity to ask questions and find out about their religions and beliefs. I wanted to know what people could do to avoid the bloodshed and destruction that resulted from the misuse of religion and the name of God. There were some common views, while others were very unique. Some answers overlapped, while others were polarizing and confusing. As a matter of habit, I did not enter into any arguments or long, drawn-out discussions, even on controversial points. Likewise, I talked to all sorts of people of different faiths, practices, professions, trades, lifestyles, income levels, ages, cultures and socioeconomic backgrounds on the same subject, bringing the topic up as a part of my casual conversations. In my travels in different parts of the world, I had many of these conversations, always making it interesting to them by touching upon the positives I could recognize in their manner of living and faith. When it came to the intricacies of their very own faiths, it was fascinating to note what some knew and what some did not.

At one point in my late fifties, I was prompted in my heart and mind to fast for forty days, entering into solitude in the wilderness for the last seven days of the fast. I did this two years in a row in order to deeply reflect upon this subject. I spent the time in quiet contemplation, meditation, prayer and worship; I sought answers from God; I asked if, in reality, there even was a God. I wanted to see what God might offer on the subject when approached through fasting and praying—a means of communication with the Holy that's much discussed among theologians and scholars. Enthused by what I was receiving and experiencing during those times, my pursuit expanded. I began seeking answers that could be simply and easily understood by a regular person regarding the following questions: What is godliness? How best to live in a godly way in different walks of life? Why and how have so many religions and faiths evolved? How many gods are there? Why does God allow certain things to keep going on, such as the followers of one faith wanting others to change theirs? How can everyone do what God wants done, which should be acceptable to all and non-controversial? Thereafter, from time to time, I went on several shorter durations of fasting and praying as I felt prompted, seeking one answer after the other.

This book is a result of the above encounters and experiences. It elucidates the various wisdoms I have received—wisdoms I feel compelled to present to the world and humanity, from the common person to the scholars and theologians, for their consideration. For a very long time in my life, whenever someone said God spoke to them, I was unsure if that person was telling the truth, or telling a lie and misusing the name of God. But I never questioned them. During my times of fasting and praying, I learned that there is God, and that God does indeed give wisdom and speak directly to or through certain people, places and events. God communicates with us in so many other ways, too, though I have found that God speaks more profoundly to those tireless seekers of the divine who do not condemn others but instead show only selfless love. Every word in this book of my own writing is what I received during those encounters. If I do not acknowledge God in this regard, I would be ungrateful. After all, when one individual does something good or gives words of encouragement or wisdom or help, isn't gratitude expressed to that person? If so, why shouldn't I be grateful to God and boldly say it was God that gave me the words of this book?

However, I request that, for the moment, you please put aside your own personal belief or unbelief in God. Come to the following with as open a mind as possible, accepting what you can, potentially adopting what you accept and contemplating that which you cannot accept. Many people write many books, and it is not necessary that everyone accepts every part of what is written. Therefore, please take whatever you feel is worthy in what you read here and leave the rest. You decide what to do then. I am convinced in my heart that most readers will find they can share their faith with others with respect and love. Indeed, I sincerely believe that every open-minded reader will derive very real benefits for themselves from others who have different beliefs, whether theists or atheists, and regardless of their socio-economic backgrounds, lifestyles and faiths. There is at least something in this book that can benefit every individual in some area of their lives, so that each one can become a better individual. Let every one of us do our part to make the world a better place to live for ourselves and others, in Peace and Joy, with Love.

CHAPTER 2

The Voice through the Ages

INTRODUCTION: WORDS ON THE WORD TO THE WORLD

In my prayers, the Voice led me to see how uniquely this panorama of religion unfolded from the Divine point of view. Our current generation is truly blessed in being able to study such a vast span of spiritual evolution, as earlier generations would never have had the knowledge or communication ability to do so.

It is with trepidation I write here that what I heard the Voice tell me may be considered a unique vision of the oneness of God and the oneness of humanity, but I believe it is worthy of consideration in your own journey towards hearing the Voice and gaining wisdom. There is the human perspective on history and spirituality, and there is the Divine perspective. What follows is what I received and understood in my prayers as the perspective of the Voice throughout history. I learned what some heard from the Voice, what some did in response to hearing and what happened to their respective cultures afterwards. Therefore, such phrases as "it is proposed" or "according to" are not often used, but rather, each religion is presented as if the experiences and wisdom they each cite are true. If this were not done, I don't believe you or I would receive the full effect of what it means to be a regular person in these particular religions. I wish to pay respect to True One God, and part of this means not condemning nor throwing suspicion on people's religious practices by insinuating that some events may not have occurred.

This book is presented as if there were a panel of common people simply explaining their religion, comfortable to express themselves without diluting their beliefs. For the sake of simplicity in this writing, I consider the word labels of *religion*, *tradition*, *faith*, or *philosophy* interchangeable. The insight and information below pertaining to each mentioned religion is primarily gained from my conversations with all these practitioners over many years, as well as from my own spiritual experiences.

There are many beliefs and practices that are common in the religions of the world: pursuit of virtue and moral codes, belief in the afterlife or some variation thereof, the felt desire for inner purification, the practice of prayer, helping the needy, respecting elders and performing various rituals to mark notable events in our lives or to act as portals to the spirit realm. This commonality is a testimony to the oneness of humanity in our mutual pursuit of one Truth. Many followers will tell you they feel a sense of peace and wonder whenever they read their scriptures or practice a ritual or worship, and this is of great value to society and to individuals alike. There can be more disagreement between worshippers within one religion than between different religions, and yet people of one religion commonly worship together. Many of the most devout of each religion are the poor, whose prayers the rich have to thank for the continued benevolence of God.

Throughout this book I have used various names for God such as: the Voice, (or just "Voice" as I would use that as my own personal endearment), God, True God, One God, True One God, Source, the Divine or Divine Consciousness, etc. and I have used the pronoun He because it is traditional. All of these names are interchangeable. I want to respect all people in all religions; respect is a common language, and I hope I have spoken it here in these pages.

As you meditate on these writings, you may see that some cultures have complementarity in their religions and philosophies, resulting in harmony for their culture; the presence of Taoism alongside Confucianism in Chinese culture is a good example. Harmony is an expression or frequency of oneness. You can hear and see harmony in nature, which itself is a reflection of the Divine. This is why some religions see all of nature as a shrine dedicated to the sacred.

If you approach spirituality and divinity from the perspective of religion, you can see the imprint of True One God in all of history, even back to early cultures. Even though some truths have been corrupted by weak and evil humans, Truth is Truth and has had to be periodically rescued by God. This is not a "find your own truth" book nor a "you can save yourself" book nor an "everybody's right" book; instead, it contains my personal reflections and understanding from my own journey to oneness. Not to split hairs, as Westerners say, but this book is not about "unity" but rather "oneness." I think of oneness as a state of being, whereas in the English language the word unity is used primarily as it relates to something mentally assented to by organizations or institutions, and its meaning can shift at the whim of individuals. I ask myself what I can learn from each religion about God and spirituality, and what inspiration and insight I can gain if I seek with a humble heart. If there is at least a remnant of divine inspiration in ANY religion, then shouldn't it be respected and revered rather than trashed? Why should I be robbed of truth because others have misused it?

Therefore, through prayerful meditation let us glean what is precious from this treasure trove of the divine encounters of humanity. Rationalism is a good tool for analysis of material facts, but it doesn't seem to be a vehicle capable of transporting Eternal Truth. Rationalism can also carry with it a fear of gullibility, which can cause a person to miss out on the uniqueness of Truth. For all these reasons, I use both my mind and spirit in this journey. I have found it fulfilling to pursue, preserve and respect divine inspiration, whatever or whoever the revelator is or was, as it is useful for daily life and for my communion with True One God. Divinely inspired words are portals into Heaven. I understand the human mouthpiece is frail, but the Divine is not. It appears to me that God is not afraid to flow through frail human vessels. It must be His good pleasure to do so, for mysterious reasons.

Aren't many of the differences between religions (and within religions) more to do with cultural traditions, rituals, practices and socioeconomic status than spirituality? Various religions of the world are discussed below, in twelve groups. There are many more, but these are meant simply to use as examples—not to be a comprehensive list. The trials, tribulations, extremists and abuses I set aside, focusing here instead on the core teachings from each of these religions—and utilizing respect, not condemnation.

INDIGENOUS SPIRITUALITY

Indigenous spirituality includes the faith-based traditions of native cultures on all continents except Antarctica, which has no indigenous population.

I have friends in Hawaii who are volcano worshipers. They consider their indigenous spirituality to be monotheistic but pay respects to the Supreme God by leaving offerings at the edge of the volcano. They believe all things are "animated" with the presence of a Supreme God; this includes not just people or things, but even our words, which are permeated with the Spirit. In their tradition of indigenous spirituality, they do not have a shaman, but in many indigenous populations shamanhood is common.

A shaman, which can be a man or a woman, is considered a healer, a leader of rituals and even a keeper of the cultural identity. Shamans have a variety of methods for contacting the spirit realm, including chants, dances and the use of hallucinogens. Through these ceremonial actions, the shaman can obtain favor with the Divine, ward off evil spirits and invite good spirits. Rituals are considered a way for anyone else to interface with the spirit realm as well, and the rituals of dancing or chanting or even the use of hallucinogens can induce a meditative state that allows one to access the spirit realm.

A common trait of many indigenous spiritualities is the veneration of ancestors. Some traditions worship the ancestors, but most simply respect them, occasionally seek communication with them (spiritism) or make offerings at special ceremonies to honor them. There are some individuals in indigenous cultures who are atheists, but this is not common. Some simply describe themselves as irreligious, not atheistic but simply choosing to not adhere to any religious practice.

There are also soul purification ceremonies that are common in these traditions, including the use of sweat lodges, fasting or ritualized bathing. Prayers are vital, particularly for a good harvest, a successful hunt, blessings for a marriage or a new baby, and especially at funerals. These are deeply important. The afterlife is looked forward to and is a place where our eternal soul goes. Most indigenous spiritual traditions have been passed down orally, though there are some cultures that use Wampum belts with beads and inscriptions to keep track of important stories and plans that need to be kept at the forefront of the people's minds. In order to create a legacy of the spiritual revelations and vital information on rituals, depictions were drawn into stone, leather and other natural materials.

This is an act of devotion to the True God or the primary deity, family and culture.

The adaptability of indigenous spirituality has made it particularly easy to incorporate into religious syncretism, i.e., combining it with other religious practices. This is why indigenous faith remains a worldwide practice, no matter what religion it ends up falling under. Indigenous spirituality permeates the culture and individual identity, perhaps more so than many other religions and faiths. As in all societies, culture influences religious practices and everyone's personal understanding of the Divine.

The indigenous peoples of North America have a rich tradition of spirituality. An especially spiritually gifted family in the Oglala Lakota tribe, with four generations of medicine men (shamans), lived in the Paha Sapa area, now modern-day Wyoming and the Black Hills of

South Dakota in the United States. From this family came a man named Hehaka Sapa, who was later named Black Elk (1863-1950).

When Black Elk was nine years old, he had a severe illness and almost died from it. During his illness, he had a very lengthy vision in which he saw multiple spirit beings that informed him of the future of his people. The spirit beings led him on a journey to see the whole earth as a series of hoops that joined as one, with a mighty tree in the center to shelter all the children of earth as one: (Below are excerpts recorded by John Niehart in his book *Black Elk Speaks*):

"...the Voice said: "Behold your nation...thenceforth your people walk in difficulties."...the people broke camp...they did not want to go, but could not stay.

... the nation's hoop was broken like a ring of smoke...the holy tree seemed dying...the Voice spoke like someone weeping: "Look there upon your nations."

... I was standing on the highest mountain of them all, round about beneath me was the whole hoop of the world...while I stood there I saw more than I can tell and I understood more than I saw; for I was seeing in a sacred manner the shapes of all things in the spirit, and the shape of all shapes as they must live together like one being. I saw that the sacred hoop of my people was one of many hoops that made one circle, wide as daylight and as starlight, and in the center grew one mighty flowering tree to shelter all the children of one mother and one father. I saw that it was holy...As I rode in through the rainbow door, there were cheering voices from all over the universe...in the cloud were faces thronging, without number, of the people yet to be."

Black Elk continued to have remarkable spiritual experiences, especially visions about the future tragedies his people would endure; but he prophesied there would ultimately be one people. He wanted to save his people from tragedy but did not live to see that happen.

However, he stood as a beacon of light for his people and the legacy of his vision still inspires.[1]

Another well-known Oglala Lakota spiritual leader, Thasunke Witko, better known as Crazy Horse (1840-1877), was a war leader and elder cousin of Black Elk. Crazy Horse also had a vision revealing the oneness of humanity; he saw a sacred tree and all the colors of humanity gathering under this tree becoming one circle.[2]

Another remarkable indigenous leader in North America, named Deganawidah, was known as the Peacemaker.[3] He was born into the Mohawk tribe and lived in the Lake Ontario area in the 1500s, a time when many of the local tribes were in competition and often fought. He became a legend in this culture due to his gift of receiving spiritual visions, especially related to the oneness of all people and how all people can live in peace. In one of his visions, he was given to know divine methods for providing peace amongst the neighboring tribes. From this vision he masterminded what the Iroquois call The Great Law of Peace, uniting five tribes into what came to be known as the Iroquois Confederacy, or the Haudenosaunee.[4] The Great Law of Peace was transmitted orally, and was also recorded with pictograms onto Wampum Belts, which would help the people remember the different agreements within the Law. This remarkable union and its laws influenced the American forefathers as they developed their ideas about democracy and wrote the US Constitution, and this influence has been officially recognized by the current government of the United States.[5]

In the history of indigenous people of the Mesoamerican civilizations there are stories of the creation recorded in their sacred text

---

[1] Neihardt, John G., *Black Elk Speaks*, (Lincoln, NE: Bison Books, 2014). Reprinted with permission from the John Neihardt Trust.

[2] https://redroadproject.com/7th-generation/.

[3] https://www.encyclopedia.com/people/literature-and-arts/european-art-1599-biographies/deganawidah#:~:text=Deganawida%20was%20instrumental%20in%20founding, credit%20Deganawida%20for%20his%20efforts.

[4] https://www.loc.gov/item/16027201/.

[5] https://www.govtrack.us/congress/bills/100/hconres331/text.

known as the *Popol Vuh* (a.k.a. the *Book of Council* or the *Mayan Book of the Dawn of Life*, which was translated from the hieroglyphic writings into Spanish and then English, and may or may not have been influenced by the religion of the Spanish invaders when translated). Quetzalcoatl, considered both a deity as well as an historical person and cultural hero, is written about as follows:

There was only immobility and silence in the darkness, in the night. Only the Creator, Tepeu, Gucamatz (a.k.a. Quetzalcoatl in the Quiche Mayan language) the Forefathers were in the water surrounded with light. They were hidden under green and blue feathers and were therefore called Gucamatz (Quetzalcoatl). By nature they were great sages and great thinkers. In this manner the sky existed and also the Heart of Heaven, which is the name of God and thus he is called.[6]

He was associated with Venus, the morning star, and also is said to have descended into Mictlan (hell) and anointed the bones of the long dead with his blood, using them to create a new race that currently inhabits the earth.

The arrival of the ruler Quetzalcoatl as an historical person in the culture was approximately 1000 years ago. Quetzalcoatl is credited with stopping the practice of human sacrifice, infusing new knowledge of agriculture, creating a calendar, elevating art and setting up an elaborate priesthood that had governing powers. After the kingdom was taken over by northern armies, Quetzalcoatl was expected to return to restore the peace and justice which marked his time in rulership. He was and is a type of messianic figure (or a sacred messenger or prophetic human) amongst some in the Mormon[7] and Bahá'í[8] faiths.

The similarities between the common beliefs and practices of these

---

[6] Goetz, Delia and Sylvanus Marley, transl., *Popol Vuh* (Los Angeles: Plantain Press, 1954) and https://www.gutenberg.org/cache/epub/56550/pg56550-images.html.

[7] Wirth, Diane E., "Questzalcoatl the Mayan Maize God, and Jesus Christ," *Journal of Mormon Studies*, Volume 11 number 1, Article 3. (https://scholarsarchive.byu.edu/jbms/vol11/iss1/3).

[8] Stockman, Robert H., *The Bahai Faith: A Guide for the Perplexed* (Bloomsbury Publishing: 2013).

indigenous traditions are quite remarkable, most notably the belief in the interconnectedness of all life, which flows naturally into the belief of the oneness of humanity.

In Africa, indigenous spirituality permeates the entire continent, including the cultures that practice monotheistic traditions such as Christianity and Islam.

West African Isese, known as the Yoruba religion, has several million followers worldwide. This religion believes there is a distant Supreme Deity with lesser gods to whom their prayers are primarily directed (for example, prayers for crops, weather and fertility). There are some similarities to other traditional religions from the nearby countries of Ghana and the Republic of Benin (such as Vodun, which later became associated with Haitian Voudon and Louisiana Voodoo). In Cuba, this evolved into Santeria and in Brazil it became Candomble Jeje. This process occurred mostly because of the African diaspora related to the slave trade. The name of the creator God, the Supreme Deity, is Olodumare. The religion has been passed down orally, though some of it has been written in a book called the *Odu Ifa*.

In the Horn of Africa (which includes Ethiopia, Somalia, Djibouti and Eritrea) thrives an ethnic religion known as Waaqeffanna. The word comes from Waaqa, which is the name for the Creator God in the Cushitic languages of the Oromo people of this region. Like the Yoruba religion, it is practiced in a syncretic fashion along with Christianity and Islam and likewise believes in a distant Supreme Deity.

Indigenous spiritual traditions have been practiced throughout history and are still currently thriving all over the globe, most prominently in Africa, Mongolia, North America, Latin America, the islands of the world, Greenland, and Australia, and continue to be passed down orally (and sometimes in written form) through the generations.[9]

---

[9] Much of the discussion regarding African Indigenous spirituality came from the following sources: https://www.britannica.com/search?query=vodou and https://www.ajol.info › ejossah › article › view and https://ejol.aau.edu.et/index.php/EJOSSAH/article/view/6195.

THE ABRAHAMIC FAITHS

"Moving into the future while walking backwards" (a proverb common to Jewish and Maori societies) allows us to see the past and carry its hard-earned wisdom into the future; this can sustain us in our life's journey. For example, we can look back to the creation story of Adam and Eve with fresh eyes, looking to apply its wisdom to our own future. The story of Adam and Eve in the Garden of Eden is well known to Jews, Christians, Muslims and the Bahá'í, as recorded in the Book of Genesis in the Jewish Tanakh. This story is viewed in varying ways—followers of certain religions regard it as materially factual, while others regard it as allegory or fiction. No matter how one sees or accepts this story, it offers some useful insight into the make-up of our spirit. While many of the interpretations may not be believed by people of these above-mentioned major faiths, the story is deeply embedded in our "spiritual genetics." Indeed, not only does the story of Adam and Eve play a role in the common history and the internalized conceptions of many in the Abrahamic Faiths, but similar stories can be found in the scriptures and literature of many other religions of the world.

The Jewish, Christian, Muslim and Bahá'í faiths all consider themselves as descendants of Adam and Eve in the lineage of Abraham, their common patriarch, who lived about four thousand years ago. Abraham was a monotheist: ". . . inasmuch as Abraham has obeyed My Voice, and kept My charge, My commandments, My laws, and My teachings." (Genesis 26:5 and Genesis 21:33). "And Abraham planted a tamarisk-tree in Beer-sheba, and called there on the name of the LORD, the Everlasting God." (JPS Tanakh).

Abraham heard from God in his prayers that he should move to another country where he would be blessed. He had an encounter with spiritual beings in his ongoing relationship with God, resulting in the creation of a covenant between God and Abraham. It so happened that God actually put Abraham to sleep during this process, because only God could empower and ratify the covenant, which was to give Abraham as many descendants as the grains of sand, though he had yet to have any children by the time he was an elderly man. God fulfilled the covenant and gave Abraham children.

What happened subsequently is a great controversy: Abraham, after God's promise, ultimately fathered two sons, Ishmael and Isaac, by two different women. Sarah, the mother of Isaac, was Abraham's first wife, and Hagar, the mother of Ishmael, was an Egyptian woman given to Sarah to be her maid. Due to some family issues—as all families have—there was a split. Hagar gave birth to Ishmael first. At Sarah's request and God's instruction, Abraham sent Hagar and Ishmael into the desert. Jews and Christians believe the promise to Abraham from God was consummated only through his wife, Sarah, and her son Isaac, and therefore her descendants are the "people of the covenant." Muslims consider that the promise was given to the first-born of Abraham's sons, which was Ishmael. Since that time there has been enmity between many members of this entire family.

The root of bitterness goes back to this time in history and will ultimately be resolved by True One God. All readers of Judaism, Christianity, Islam and the Bahá'í faith will recognize this is an oversimplification of the events, but this is not the place to resolve the controversy. To be sure, there are some serious issues at hand, including, but not limited to, the inheritance expected by the descendants in these faiths (Abraham is considered a prophet and would therefore pass down what he received from God, whether spiritual blessings or land and resources). Additionally, there is the aspect of the Egyptian contribution to the lineage, given that Hagar was Egyptian. Egypt is clearly important to God as it figures prominently in the Jewish Tanakh as a place of both provision and bondage for the Jews. Also, Jesus was Jewish and, and as recorded in the Christian Bible, was taken to Egypt to protect him from the evil King Herod. Herod had been told a Jewish king had been born in Bethlehem and, feeling his own authority would be threatened, he was seeking to kill him.

And for the inhabitants of Egypt there is the promise of a visitation from God. In the Jewish Tanakh it says:

19 In that day shall there be an altar to the LORD in the midst of the land of Egypt, and a pillar at the border thereof to the LORD. 20 And it shall be for a sign and for a witness unto the LORD of hosts in the land of Egypt; for they shall cry unto the LORD because of the oppressors, and He will send them a saviour, and a defender, who will deliver them. 21 And the LORD shall make Himself known to Egypt, and the Egyptians shall know the LORD in that day; yea, they shall worship with sacrifice and offering, and shall vow a vow unto the LORD, and shall perform it. 22 And the LORD will smite Egypt, smiting and healing; and they shall return unto the LORD, and He will be entreated of them, and will heal them. 23 In that day shall there be a highway out of Egypt to Assyria, and the Assyrian shall come into Egypt, and the Egyptian into Assyria; and the Egyptians shall worship with the Assyrians. 24 In that day shall Israel be the third with Egypt and with Assyria, a blessing in the midst of the earth; 25 for that the LORD of hosts hath blessed him, saying: 'Blessed be Egypt My people and Assyria the work of My hands, and Israel Mine inheritance.' [10]

JUDAISM[11]

(In the following section, the name of God is spelled as G-d out of respect for tradition as told to me by the Jewish people who taught me about Judaism. This is the preferred method of writing the name of G-d for some Jews and so it is honored here.)

Regarding the development of the Jewish religion, the descendants of Abraham that originated from Sarah and her son, Isaac, ultimately ended up in slavery in Egypt until they were delivered by G-d via Moses, a Hebrew[12] raised in the Egyptian royal household. Moses had

---

[10] Isaiah 19:19-25 (JPS Tanakh 1917).

[11] Much of this description is compiled from the following websites: https://ebible.org/study/?w1=bible&t1=local%3Aengjps&v1=JN1_1; https://www.chabad.org/library/article_cdo/aid/170308/jewish/What-Is-Kabbalah.htm; https://www.gutenberg.org/cache/epub/8294/pg8294-images.html; https://www.britannica.com/topic/Judaism

[12] The traditional terms of "Hebrew," "Israelite" or "Jew" depend on the time you are referring to in history.

developed an ongoing personal relationship with G-d through prayer, just as Abraham had. After the liberation of the Israelites from slavery in Egypt via a series of miraculous examples of the protectiveness of G-d, Moses received the Ten Commandments from G-d. Abraham was known for living according to God's laws, and through Moses, God offered these laws in a simplified form. These Ten Commandments were remarkable in their clarity and are widely known and respected throughout history and all over the globe. Unlike other codes of law in other cultures of their time, the laws of Moses emphasized forgiveness and virtue. The Ten Commandments are the most famous of the contributions of the Jewish faith.

This monotheistic faith has been carried down through prophets. A number of these prophets wrote books detailing their spiritual experiences in prayer, detailing how G-d showed them events and people that were to come, offered them wisdom and teachings on how to live life, and transmitted to them special words of prayer and praise to G-d.

The Ten Commandments are as follows:[13]

And G-d spoke all these words, saying: I am the LORD thy G-d, who brought thee out of the land of Egypt, out of the house of bondage.

-Thou shalt have no other gods before Me.

-Thou shalt not make unto thee a graven image, nor any manner of likeness, of anything that is in heaven above, or that is in the earth beneath, or that is in the water under the earth; thou shalt not bow down unto them, nor serve them; for I the LORD thy G-d am a jealous G-d, visiting the iniquity of the fathers upon the children unto the third and fourth generation of them that hate Me; and showing mercy unto the thousandth generation of them that love Me and keep My commandments.

-Thou shalt not take the name of the LORD thy G-d in vain; for the LORD will not hold him guiltless that taketh His name in vain.

-Remember the sabbath day, to keep it holy. Six days shalt thou labour,

---

[13] Exodus 20:1-20 (LXX).

and do all thy work; but the seventh day is a sabbath unto the LORD thy G-d, in it thou shalt not do any manner of work, thou, nor thy son, nor thy daughter, nor thy man-servant, nor thy maid-servant, nor thy cattle, nor thy stranger that is within thy gates; for in six days the LORD made heaven and earth, the sea, and all that in them is, and rested on the seventh day; wherefore the LORD blessed the sabbath day, and hallowed it.

-Honour thy father and thy mother, that thy days may be long upon the land which the LORD thy G-d giveth thee.

-Thou shalt not murder.

-Thou shalt not commit adultery.

-Thou shalt not steal.

-Thou shalt not bear false witness against thy neighbour.

-Thou shalt not covet thy neighbour's house; thou shalt not covet thy neighbour's wife, nor his man-servant, nor his maid-servant, nor his ox, nor his ass, nor any thing that is thy neighbour's.

And all the people perceived the thunderings, and the lightnings, and the voice of the horn, and the mountain smoking; and when the people saw it, they trembled, and stood afar off. And they said unto Moses: 'Speak thou with us, and we will hear; but let not G-d speak with us, lest we die.' And Moses said unto the people: 'Fear not; for G-d is come to prove you, and that His fear may be before you, that ye sin not.' And the people stood afar off; but Moses drew near unto the thick darkness where G-d was.[14]

On multiple occasions, the practice of worshipping man-made idols derailed the Israelites (and well-meaning modern westerners alike). Even though some would say people simply use physical objects as a "point of contact" to direct their mind to the one G-d, there have still been occasions that putting an idol, such as self-reliance or materialism, between them and G-d causes a disconnect. It is that disconnect that grieves G-d.

Moses continued a life of prayer and meditation as he led his people through the wilderness. In a series of visions, he saw into the courts of

[14] https://ebible.org/engjps/EXO20.htm

Heaven; from these visions he supervised the construction of a portable temple called the Tabernacle. It gave the children of Israel a way they could approach G-d, especially since they had declined to go up into the mountain to directly commune with G-d as Moses had done. This Tabernacle had an outer court and an inner court where the people were to approach the Presence of G-d with awe and praise and love. This was followed by an area for animal sacrifice to atone for their sin ("atonement with it upon the altar for your souls...") according to the Jewish law;[15] and then on into the "Holy of Holies," covered by a veil, where the tangible presence of G-d rested and was accessed only by the priests who were praying and interceding for people.

Throughout Jewish scripture and within Hebrew society, the concept of a Messiah or "Moshiach" can be found—describing the one who will be anointed by G-d to be a liberator/savior of the people. This concept is prominent in some Jewish circles of thought but of marginal concern in others. The expectation of a moshiach has been behind many persecutions of the Jews throughout history, from the time of Moses to the story of King Herod as told in the New Testament.

The primary Jewish Scriptures, the Torah (the teachings of Moses), the Nevi'im (the books of the prophets), and the Ketuvim (Psalms and wisdom literature) are commonly referred to as the "Tanakh," an acronym of these names. These scriptures have provided cohesiveness for this religion to spread globally.

There are mystics in the history of Judaism. Many would call David a mystic due to his intensely spiritual poetry and songs of adoration in the book of Psalms. As read in the book of Genesis, Enoch, a Hebrew patriarch from the seventh generation of descendants of Adam, was noted to have such an intimate walk with G-d that he simply walked off the earth into Heaven. He wrote of many visions of Heavenly beings and future events and was quoted by Saul, the Jewish scholar who later became Paul in the New Testament. The book of Enoch was used in

---

[15] Leviticus 17:11 (DRB): "Because the life of the flesh is in the blood: and I have given it to you, that you may make atonement with it upon the altar for your souls, and the blood may be for an expiation (cleansing from wrongdoing) of the soul."

the Hebrew culture for a time as Hekholath (mystical) literature. It fell out of popularity in the mainstream Jewish community after the second century but remains in the Beta Israel Ethiopian Jewish scriptures. Kabballah is a form of Jewish mysticism that became popular in the twelfth century. The book of Zohar is its primary text and discusses such things as the nature of souls and of G-d and the origin and structure of the universe. Messianic Jews are those that have continued the practice of Judaism and follow the teachings of Jesus, considering Jesus Christ to be the Moshiach of their soul.

The covenantal relationship with G-d is a unique element in Judaism. It is considered by some to be the backbone of the Jewish faith, contributing to the cohesiveness and resilience of Jewish culture over time, even when its people have been spread across the globe and lived within other societies.

CHRISTIANITY

More than two thousand years ago, in a town called Nazareth in Judea, a Jewish woman named Maryam (Mary) was visited by the angel Gabriel and told she would conceive a child by the Holy Spirit of God, though she was a virgin.

He will be great and will be called the Son of the Most High. The Lord God will give him the throne of his father David, and he will reign over the house of Jacob forever. There will be no end to his Kingdom… for nothing spoken by God is impossible.[16]

Joseph, to whom Mary was betrothed, was visited by an angel as well, who told him not to be worried, and to take Mary as his wife: "…for that which is conceived in her is of the Holy Spirit. She shall give birth to a son. You shall name him Yeshua, for it is he who shall save his people from their sins."[17]

Mary and Joseph traveled to Bethlehem where she gave birth

---

[16] Luke 1:32-33, 37 (WEB).

[17] Matthew 1:20-21.

"...and laid him in a feeding trough, because there was no room for them in the inn." After returning to their home in Nazareth, Jesus grew in favor with God and his community and enjoyed life as a carpenter's son.

When he was about thirty years old, Jesus went to the Jordan River to be baptized, "to fulfill all righteousness" and be an example. John the Baptist said: "Behold, the Lamb of God, who takes away the sin of the world!"[18] The sky was opened and the Holy Spirit descended in the form of a dove; then a voice came out of the sky, saying: "You are my beloved Son. In you I am well pleased."[19] After being baptized and filled with the Holy Spirit of God, Jesus went into the wilderness for forty days to pray and fast, during which time he endured the temptations of evil and prepared for his ministry.

Jesus selected twelve disciples to travel with him and teach, performing many miracles and healings. On at least two occasions he multiplied scant supplies of food to feed the thousands of people who had gathered to hear him teach. He taught the Beatitudes: "Blessed are the peacemakers, for they shall be called children of God."[20]

Some folks were joyful and healed, but the religious establishment was not. Many of the religious leaders tested Jesus, asking him what they thought were difficult questions. One asked him, "What is the greatest commandment?" He responded:

The greatest is: "Hear, Israel, the Lord our God, the Lord is one. You shall love the Lord your God with all your heart, with all your soul, with all your mind, and with all your strength." This is the first commandment. The second is like this: "You shall love your neighbor as yourself." There is no other commandment greater than these.[21]

Some of the things He taught were hard for the people to accept, including the notion that the worship of God was about far more than meaningless rituals.

---

[18] John 1:29.

[19] Luke 1:22.

[20] Matthew 5:9

[21] Mark 12: 29-31 (World Messianic Bible).

...the true worshippers will worship the Father in spirit and truth, for the Father seeks such to be his worshippers. God is spirit and those who worship him must worship in spirit and truth.[22]

You have heard that it was said, "You shall love your neighbor and hate your enemy." But I tell you, love your enemies, bless those who curse you, do good to those who hate you, and pray for those who mistreat you and persecute you that you may be children of your Father who is in heaven. For if you love those who love you, what reward do you have?[23]

For God so loved the world that He gave His only begotten Son that whoever believes in Him should not perish but have eternal life. For God did not send His Son into the world to condemn the world, but that the world through Him might be saved.[24]

Many of his followers had particularly tragic and traumatized backgrounds. One such follower was a woman, Mary (not His mother), who expressed her intense love and gratitude toward Him, for His unconditional love, by washing and anointing his feet. She broke open an expensive alabaster vessel of oil to pour on His feet and wiped his feet with her hair and her tears of gratitude. Jesus rebuked the others for their condescending behavior towards her and said:

She has done a good work for me. For you always have the poor with you, but you don't always have me. For in pouring this ointment on my body, she did it to prepare me for burial...[25]

On love and joy, He taught:

Even as the Father has loved me, I also have loved you. (Abide) Remain in my love. If you keep my commandments, you will (abide) remain in my love, even as I have kept my Father's commandments and abide in His love. I have spoken these things to you, that my joy may remain in you, and that your joy may be made full. This is my commandment, that you love one

---

[22] John 4:23-24.

[23] Matthew 5:39-47.

[24] John 3:16-17.

[25] Matthew 26:10-13.

another, even as I have loved you. Greater love has no one than this, that someone lay down his life for his friends.[26]

Jesus informed his disciples that he came to give his life and expected to die as a result of the persecutions he faced, but that he would send the "Helper" (a.k.a. "the Comforter"), the Spirit of truth. Prior to his arrest he went to the Garden of Gethsemane and prayed so intensely he sweated blood:

...that they may all be one; even as you, Father, are in me, and I in you, that they also may be one in us; that the world may believe that you sent me. I made known to them your name and will make it known; that the love with which you loved me may be in them, and I in them.[27]

Ultimately, his persecutors charged Him with blasphemy and captured him as he was betrayed by one of his disciples, Judas. Jesus was put in prison, questioned, beaten, and then crucified. At the time Jesus gave up His spirit and died, there was an earthquake, and many were raised from the dead. The veil in the temple that had separated all but the priests from the Holy of Holies was torn in two, demonstrating that Jesus forged the way for all people to connect straight to the holiness of God. His crucifixion was on the day of the Passover feast. Passover is a Jewish holy day commemorating the application of blood on the door posts of the Jews in Egypt so that the angel of death would "pass over" them at the time of the plagues before their exodus and deliverance from Egypt. After he had died, his body was placed in a tomb and sealed by a large rock.

On the third day of Passover, the Feast of First Fruits, when three women went to check on the body, two angels appeared and told them Jesus had been resurrected as He had said He would be. Jesus was raised up by the Holy Spirit of God as a model or manifested archetype for all who would believe and follow him into oneness with God.

One hundred twenty disciples tarried in Jerusalem as instructed by Jesus before His death, and fifty days after Passover, as they were

---

[26] John 15:9-13 (WEB).

[27] John 17:20-26.

celebrating the Feast of Weeks (Shavuot), which commemorates the reception of the Ten Commandments by Moses on Mount Sinai, they experienced a spiritual encounter like no other. They described it as a mighty rushing wind and a fire in the room alighting on each person, and as they prayed they began to speak in other tongues. This was the fulfillment of the word of Jesus that the "Helper" would come. They went out into the streets to tell of Jesus' teachings on love, forgiveness, and redemption by way of his death, burial, and resurrection. At this event about three thousand people were added to the group of believers, such was the effect of the empowerment of the Holy Spirit in them. Subsequently, Jesus appeared to the disciples and others in the area, letting them know He would always be with them, and gave them the Great Commission to spread the good news they had learned. Then he encouraged them, and

...as they were looking, he was taken up, and a cloud received him out of their sight. While they were looking steadfastly into the sky as he went, behold, two men stood by them in white clothing, who also said, "You men of Galilee, why do you stand looking into the sky? This Jesus, who was received up from you into the sky, will come back in the same way as you saw him going into the sky."[28]

Soon thereafter, a man named Saul, a Jewish scholar and former persecutor of early Christians, had an experience on the road to Damascus in which he had a blinding vision of Jesus, who asked him, "Why do you persecute me?" Saul's heart was transformed, and he went on to teach about Jesus. Saul experienced Jesus as a liberator/savior or a Moshiach of the soul, resetting human righteousness from within. Saul used the Hebrew scriptures extensively in his teaching, citing that it contained the prophetic infrastructure needed to withstand the weight of the impact of Jesus coming as Moshiach or Messiah.

Saul (also called Paul) taught that Jesus gave His life for all people, and when a person gives Jesus their life, then the life you now live belongs to Christ, who inhabits and lives through you.

---

[28] Acts 1:8-11 (WMB).

17 Therefore if anyone is in Christ, he is a new creation. The old things have passed away. Behold…all things have become new. 18 But all things are of God, who reconciled us to himself through Jesus Christ, and gave to us the ministry of reconciliation; 19 namely, that God was in Christ reconciling the world to himself, not reckoning to them their trespasses, and having committed to us the word of reconciliation.[29]

John, one of Jesus' disciples, wrote much on the subject of love:

We know and have believed the love which God has for us. God is love, and he who remains in love remains in God, and God remains in him… We love him, because he first loved us. If a man says, "I love God," and hates his brother, he is a liar; for he who doesn't love his brother whom he has seen, how can he love God whom he has not seen?[30]

The last book of the New Testament, the book of Revelation, is a series of visions with instructions from Jesus Christ written down by the prophet John of Patmos. An angel appeared carrying a message from Jesus about the "end of the age" and his plan for bringing people into oneness with God:

"I am the Alef and the Tav, the First and the Last, the Beginning and the End." Blessed are those who do his commandments, that they may have the right to the tree of life, and may enter in by the gates into the city. Outside are the dogs, the sorcerers, the sexually immoral, the murderers, the idolaters, and everyone who loves and practices falsehood. "I, Yeshua, have sent my angel to testify these things to you for the assemblies. I am the root and the offspring of David, the Bright and Morning Star." The Spirit and the bride say, "Come!" He who hears, let him say, "Come!" He who is thirsty, let him come. He who desires, let him take the water of life freely.[31]

This passage reveals the right to eat from the Tree of Life, as written

---

[29] 2 Corinthians 5:17-21 (WEB).

[30] 1 John 4:13-20 (WEB).

[31] Book of Revelation 22:13-17 (HNV).

The following sources were used for much of the above discussion: https://www.britannica.com/topic/Christianity and https://www.worldhistory.org/christianity/

about in the Jewish Tanakh Genesis 3:22-24 (this was after Adam and Eve had eaten from the Tree of the Knowledge of Good and Evil, against God's command): *22 And the LORD God said: 'Behold, the man is become as one of us, to know good and evil; and now, lest he put forth his hand, and take also of the tree of life, and eat, and live for ever.' 23 Therefore the LORD God sent him forth from the garden of Eden, to till the ground from whence he was taken. 24 So He drove out the man; and He placed at the east of the garden of Eden the cherubim, and the flaming sword which turned every way, to keep the way to the tree of life.* This "right to the Tree of Life" is the promise of eternal life in the spirit and oneness with God—what some would call the essence of the message and purpose of Christ and his earthly life.

As the centuries went by, the Christian religion grew rapidly, but Christians were being persecuted as well. These persecutions began to decline after the Roman emperor Constantine became a believer in Christ and participated in creating the Edict of Milan, which gave Christianity legal status and protection throughout the Roman Empire.

Many reformations within Christianity have occurred over the two millennia since the life of Jesus. The scriptures known as the Holy Bible, in its various compilations, were assembled from the Hebrew texts, the writings of Jesus' direct disciples, Paul, and others as well. The Ethiopian and Eritrean Orthodox Tewahedo Church scriptures include the books of Enoch.

ISLAM[32]

Muhammed ibn Abdullah ibn Abd al-Muttalib ibn Hashim (peace be upon him) was born nearly fourteen hundred years ago in the city of Mecca in Arabia. His father was a tribal leader who died around the time of his son's birth, and his mother died when he was a small child. Therefore, he was raised by his grandfather and uncle. He grew up

---

[32] Much of this discussion is compiled from the following website:
https://www.history.com/topics/religion/islam.

during a time when Arabian culture included a mix of polytheists, Jews, Christians, Zoroastrians and others.

Muhammed (peace be upon him) practiced a form of monotheism known as Hanif, and avoided polytheism. When he was about forty years old, he had a vision in which he saw the archangel, Gabriel. He continued to have further visitations, all of which pointed to the existence of one God, an idea counter to the belief and practice of some of the surrounding polytheistic tribes.

He began to teach people in his community about the oneness of God (Allah, in Arabic, meaning "glorified and exalted") and gathered many followers. At one point, he and some of his followers relocated to Medina to escape persecution from the polytheistic tribes who were in power in Mecca. Intermittent fighting between those tribes continued however, so Muhammed (peace be upon him) gathered about ten thousand faithful soldiers and took over Mecca.

The visitations from Gabriel continued over the course of about twenty-three years. His closest companions served as scribes as he recited these revelations, writing them down so they could be shared with his followers. A few years after the death of Muhammed (peace be upon him), these writings were assembled, and a standard compilation (called the Qur'an) was completed about twelve to fifteen years after his death. Faithful Muslims consider these writings to be the literal words of Allah (glorified and exalted) and are intended to guide people and to be the final revelation to humanity through Muhammed (peace be upon his name), the last prophet.

The Five Pillars of Islam are the basic obligatory acts or practices for all Muslims. These are words of guidance noted at various places in the Qur'an and can be described as follows:

1 – Accepting the foundational statement of faith, or Shahada, which can be found in the eighteenth verse of the third chapter of the Qur'an, called Surah Ali 'Imran: "There is no god but He: That is the witness of Allah, His angels, and those endued with knowledge, standing firm

on justice. There is no god but He, the Exalted in Power, the Wise."[33]

The second aspect requiring acceptance is, "Muhammed is the messenger of God." If a person recites this phrase with faith, then that person becomes a Muslim, a follower of the religion of Islam. The word Islam means submission to Allah (glorified and exalted).

2 – Pray five times a day, facing Mecca. This includes reciting the opening chapter of the Qur'an, called Surah al-Fatihah:

In the name of Allah, Most Gracious, Most Merciful.
Praise be to Allah, the Cherisher and Sustainer of the worlds;
Most Gracious, Most Merciful;
Master of the Day of Judgment.
Thee do we worship, and Thine aid we seek.
Show us the straight way,
The way of those on whom Thou hast bestowed Thy Grace,
those whose [portion] is not wrath, and who go not astray.[34]

Men will gather in a mosque at noonday prayer on Fridays; women are welcome but not obliged to participate in the prayer.

3 – Giving alms. Muslims donate a portion of their money to help the poor and to build mosques and other charitable projects.

4 – Fasting. During daylight hours of Ramadan (the ninth month of the Islamic lunar calendar) all healthy adult Muslims abstain from food and drink in order to share in the lack experienced by the hungry and to remind themselves of the provisions of Allah (glorified and exalted).

5 – Pilgrimage. Every able-bodied Muslim who has the financial capability must make at least one visit to Mecca to visit the Ka'ba, a

---

[33] Qur'an 3:18 (trans. A. Yusuf Ali).

[34] Qur'an 1:1-7 (trans. A. Yusuf Ali).

structure at the center of the Haram Mosque in Mecca, built by Abraham.

There are many words of guidance in the Quran about practical daily life, including the advice of Abraham and Jacob to their children: "And this was the legacy that Abraham left to his sons, and so did Jacob; 'Oh my sons! Allah hath chosen the Faith for you; then die not except in the Faith of Islam.'"[35]

Muhammed (peace be upon him) is a descendant of Abraham (peace be upon him) through Ishmael whose mother was Hagar. Abraham is mentioned frequently throughout the Quran.

Another passage encourages all humble souls to prayerful submission:

They fall down on their faces in tears, and it increases their [earnest] humility.
Say: "Call upon Allah, or call upon Rahman[36]: by whatever name ye call upon Him, [it is well]: for to Him belong the Most Beautiful Names.[37]

Another offers general family life guidance:

Thy Lord hath decreed that ye worship none but Him, and that ye be kind to parents. Whether one or both of them attain old age in thy life, say not to them a word of contempt, nor repel them, but address them in terms of honour.
And, out of kindness, lower to them the wing of humility, and say: "My Lord! bestow on them thy Mercy even as they cherished me in childhood."[38]

---

[35] Ibid 2:132.

[36] Rahman is another name of God, meaning "gracious and merciful."

[37] Ibid 17:109-111.

[38] Ibid 17:23-24.

There is a significant portion of the Quran devoted to the afterlife and the last judgment:

At length, when there comes the Deafening Noise,
That Day shall a man flee from his own brother,
And from his mother and his father,
And from his wife and his children.
Each one of them, that Day, will have enough concern [of his own] to
make him indifferent to the others.
Some faces that Day will be beaming,
Laughing, rejoicing.
And other faces that Day will be dust-stained,
Blackness will cover them:
Such will be the Rejecters of Allah, the doers of iniquity.[39]

The religion of Islam spread throughout the Arabian Peninsula, then outward from there. Very shortly after the death of Muhammed (peace be upon him), there was a split in his followers over the question of who would succeed him. Most of the followers (who became the Sunni) wanted to decide as a community, but others (who became the Shia or Shi'ite) wanted one of his family members to lead—Ali, who was married to Fatimah, the daughter of Muhammed (peace be upon him). A war broke out between the two factions, and the Sunnis won after much loss of life. The Sunnis and Shia have never reunited.

It is from the Shi'ites that the story of the 12th Imam arises. He is known as the "Hidden Imam" and is the Mahdi or Messianic figure. This group became known as the Twelver Shi'ites and is the group from which Babism sprang, which became the Bahá'í Faith.

The mystical expression of Islam is known as Sufism. The name likely refers to the wool blanket worn by early Sufi ascetics ("suf" meaning wool). The most important concepts in Sufism are repentance, having a relationship with a spiritual guide (the Shaykh), poverty (not being possessed by possessions), dealing with evil tendencies (nafs), self-mortification, continuously thinking about and trusting in Allah

[39] Ibid 80:33-42.

(glorified and exalted) and the practice of meditation. Sufis consider this journey the means to become united with Allah (glorified and exalted).

Sufis are known for their missionary activities and charitable acts, and they have greatly contributed to the spread of Islam throughout Turkey, Iran, Iraq, Egypt, and into African countries such as Senegal, Algeria and Morocco.[40]

Some of the greatest contributions of Sufism have been through poetry and music written from their perspective of divine union. One of the earliest Sufi mystics was Rabia Basri. A poet, she lived in the 700s and is considered one of the most prominent Qalandars (a title that honors a Sufi that is highly gifted spiritually). Other writers admired by Sufis are Ibn Al-Arabi (author of the poem "A Garden Among the Flames") and Baba Kuhi of Shiraz and Jalāl Al-Dīn Muhammed Rūmī (known in the Western world simply as "Rumi").

Thus writes Jalāl Al-Dīn Muhammed Rūmī:

The song of the spheres in their revolutions
Is what men sing with lute and voice.
As we all are members of Adam,
We have heard these melodies in Paradise.
Though earth and water have cast their veil upon us,
We retain faint reminiscences of these heavenly songs;
But while we are thus shrouded by gross earthly veils,
How can the tones of the dancing spheres reach us?[41]

The following is a translation of a poem by Baba Kuhi of Shiraz (died 1050):

---

[40] https://www.britannica.com/topic/Sufism

[41] E. H. Whinfield, 1914 abridged translation of the Masnavī, p. 182. Public domain; https://www.gutenberg.org/cache/epub/67388/pg67388-images.html

In the market, in the cloister—only God I saw.
In the valley and on the mountain—only God I saw.
Him I have seen beside me oft in tribulation;
In favour and in fortune—only God I saw.
In prayer and fasting, in praise and contemplation,
In the religion of the Prophet—only God I saw.
Neither soul nor body, accident nor substance,
Qualities nor causes—only God I saw.
I opened mine eyes and by the light of His face around me
In all the eye discovered—only God I saw.
Like a candle I was melting in His fire:
Amidst the flames outflashing—only God I saw.
Myself with mine own eyes I saw most clearly,
But when I looked with God's eyes—only God I saw.
I passed away into nothingness, I vanished,
And lo, I was the All-living—only God I saw.[42]

THE BAHÁ'Í FAITH[43]

Ali Muhammad, a direct descendant of the prophet Muhammad, was born to a Shia Muslim family in Shiraz, Iran in 1819. They were members of Twelver Shi'ism, which holds that the Imams were and are spiritual and political successors to Muhammad, free from sin, infallible, and chosen by divine decree, and that the 12th Imam, a descendant of Muhammad, is the Mahdi (the guide) who will return at the End of Times, just before the arrival of Jesus, to rid the world of evil. They further followed the teachings of a mystical sub-sect of the Twelver doctrine called Shaykhism.

---

[42] The Mystics of Islam, by Reynold Nicholson, 1914. Original publication: United Kingdom: G. Bell & Sons Ltd, 1914

[43] The following description is compiled from the following website: https://www.bahai.org/beliefs/universal-peace/articles-resources/from-unfoldment-world-civilization.

From the age of twenty-five, Ali Muhammad spent several years writing a great deal on his beliefs, including the concept of progressive revelation in religion, meaning the ongoing renewal of religious thought. He also recommended repeal of many Islamic laws, promoted unity and equality of people, and went to great lengths to emphasize the importance of education for all. He became known as the "Bab" (meaning "gate") and his followers were called "Babis." He predicted another messianic figure would come after him to usher in global unity and peace. He was admired by the poor of his day because he emphasized ethics, social justice and investigations of truth which challenged corruption. But the orthodox government and clergy arrested him, and he was executed along with thousands of his followers in 1850. His most famous writing was the Persian Bayan, which told of the coming arrival of the Promised One and remains a primary scripture for the Bahá'í today.

This monotheistic, messianic faith began to grow, eventually attracting a follower known as Mírzá Husayn Alí Núrí, who had been imprisoned for following the teachings of the Bab. During one of his imprisonments, it was revealed to him that he was the Promised One foretold by the Bab and referred to in Muslim and Hebrew scriptures. In the Bahá'í faith, the Bab is considered a sort of "forerunner" to the Promised One, much as John the Baptist was considered a forerunner to Jesus. In 1848, Mírzá Husayn took the title of Bahá'u'lláh, meaning the glorification of God, and wrote that he was one of the Manifestations of God—the line of High Prophets sent by God to reveal God's Divine Essence. These Prophets include Adam, Noah, Krishna, Zoroaster, Abraham, Ishmael, Moses, Buddha, Jesus, Muhammed, Bab, and finally, Bahá'u'lláh.

Bahá'u'lláh spent most of his later years imprisoned and was a very prolific writer. In addition to the Bayan of the Bab, the main scripture of the Bahá'í is the Kitab-i-Aqdas (The Most Holy Book) which lays out the laws of God as received by Bahá'u'lláh in his prayers. In his copious letters to his son, 'Abdu'l-Bahá, he wrote of his revelations of a new world order, one government, one language to be spoken and one religion.

Bahá'u'lláh's great-grandson, Shoghi Effendi, a prolific writer as well, emphasized the importance of the unity of the followers of the Bahá'í faith. He distinguished two forms of the essential Bahá'í Covenant, or "Agreement with God:" the Greater Covenant and the Lesser Covenant. According to the Greater Covenant, each of the Manifestations of God promises their followers that a new Manifestation will come after them (about every thousand years) and asks them to accept the new Manifestation in this process of progressive revelation when it occurs. The Lesser Covenant asks the Bahá'í faithful to also accept the successor that is chosen by the Manifestation, as well as the following successors chosen by the Bahá'í governing body; this was meant to prevent splits and disunity amongst the followers so that no individual should be permitted to claim special understanding.[44]

In his letter of 11 March, 1936, published under the title, "The Unfoldment of World Civilization," Shoghi Effendi outlined a vision of the future of humankind, declaring that diversity of religion and race should no longer be.

Bahá'ís continue to follow the teachings of Bahá'u'lláh and are practicing in over two hundred countries around the world; their central location is the Bahá'í World Centre in Haifa, Israel. The Bahá'í faith is still persecuted in Iran to this day. The primary scriptures are the Bayan of Bab and the writings of Bahá'u'lláh, especially the Kitab-i-Aqdas.

ZOROASTRIANISM

There was a young man, Zarathushtra Spitama (Zoroaster is the Greek rendering of his name), who lived in what is now modern-day greater-Iran about 3500 years ago. He had a vision of a Heavenly Being and began a life of quiet prayer. He subsequently had a series of visions showing him that there is only one True God, rather than the pantheon of gods worshipped in the ancient Middle East during his time. He became a religious reformer, and his writings helped people understand

---

[44] https://bahaipedia.org/Covenant#Lesser_Covenant.

that evil is not the opposite of God but rather the lack of light from God in a person.[45]

Zoroaster wrote many beautiful hymns of praise and worship of the One True God, Ahura Mazda, Creator God. By the sharing of these visions from his prayer, Zoroaster's hymns gave words to people to sing back to True One God. Many of his hymns are intensely devotional in nature and speak of the beauty realm of God. Zoroaster wrote about righteous living and the understanding that good triumphs over evil—which is common modern thinking to us now but was a fresh revelation for civilization at that time.

Zoroastrians are known for practicing "good thoughts, good words and good deeds." Worship is commonly done in front of a continuous fire as a point of focus to worship the One God. There is no worship of the actual fire, something frequently misunderstood. One went to Heaven if righteous and good in this life, and to hell if not. Zoroastrianism is a moralistic religion, and its creed emphasizes that "Righteousness is the best!" About 1400 years ago, after the Arab invasion, the Zoroastrians were severely persecuted and therefore migrated gradually to the Gujarat area of India. They are now known as the Parsis.[46]

The primary Zoroastrian scripture is called the Zend-Avesta, including the principal text, the Yasna, which contains the five Gathas, or hymns, ascribed to Zoroaster himself. Other books compiled by later authors commenting on Zoroastrianism are the Denkard (Dk) and the Bundahishn, as well as others. Some key tenets and prayers from these scriptures follow.

...the desire of Ahura Mazda (the One True God) from people is this: "Know me," for he knows: "If they know me, everyone will follow me." The desire of Angra Mainyu (evil) is this: "Do not know me," for he knows: "If they know me no one will follow me."[47]

---

[45] https://www.britannica.com/topic/Zoroastrianism.

[46] https://www.britannica.com/topic/Zoroastrianism.

[47] Dk 6:31 (trans. Mills) (https://avesta.org/denkard/dk6s.htm#v27). Reprinted with permission of Joseph Peterson.

Angra Mainyu (evil) is best fought by joy; despondency is a symptom of his victory.[48]

As the soul is thus not all, but is in the world for a period for maintaining the body, it is necessary to walk with such circumspection as if one were without shoes, and the whole of this world were full of snakes, scorpions, noxious reptiles, and thorns, and one's fear were: "Let not the reptiles bite me, or the thorns penetrate me."[49]

In Zoroastrian theology, paying attention is personified as Sraosha (Hearkening).[50]

...Thou, O Mazda, in the beginning didst create the Individual and the Individuality, through Thy Spirit, and powers of understanding... Thou didst make life clothed with the body... (Thou madest) actions and teachings, whereby one may exercise one's convictions at one's free-will...[51]

A prayer for sanctity and its benefits:

I pray with benedictions for a benefit, and for the good, even for the entire creation of the holy (and the clean); I beseech for them for the (generation which is) now alive, for that which is just coming into life, and for that which shall be hereafter. And (I pray for that) sanctity which leads to prosperity, and which has long afforded shelter, which goes on hand in hand with it, which joins it in its walk, and of itself becoming its close companion as it delivers forth its precepts, bearing every form of healing virtue which comes to us in waters, appertains to cattle, or is found in plants, and overwhelming, all the harmful malice of the Daevas, (and their servants) who might harm this dwelling and its lord, bringing good gifts,

---

[48] https://www.avesta.org/zfaq.html. Reprinted with permission.

[49] Dk 6:b47 (trans. Shaked) (https://www.avesta.org/zfaq.html). Reprinted with permission.

[50] https://www.avesta.org/zfaq.html. Reprinted with permission.

[51] Y 31:11 (trans. Mills) (https://www.avesta.org/yasna/index.html#y35). Reprinted with permission.

and better blessings, given very early, and later (gifts), leading to successes, and for a long time giving shelter. And so the greatest, and the best, and most beautiful benefits of sanctity fall likewise to our lot.

For the sacrifice, homage, propitiation, and the praise of the Bountiful Immortals, for the bringing prosperity to this abode, and for the prosperity of the entire creation of the holy, and the clean, (and as for this, so) for the opposition of the entire evil creation. (And I pray for this) as I praise through Righteousness, I who am beneficent, those who are (likewise of a better mind).[52]

May'st Thou, O Ahura Mazda! reign at Thy will, and with a saving rule over Thine own creatures, and render Ye the holy (man) also a sovereign at his will over waters, and over plants, and over all the clean and sacred (creatures) which contain the seed of Righteousness. Strip ye the wicked of all power![53]

In order that our minds may be delighted, and our souls the best, let our bodies be glorified as well, and let them; O Mazda! go likewise openly (unto Heaven) as the best world of the saints as devoted to Ahura, and accompanied by Asha Vahishta (who is Righteousness the Best), and the most beautiful! And may we see Thee, and may we, approaching, come around about Thee, and attain to entire companionship with Thee!
Ashem Vohu...[54]

JAINISM[55]

Jainism began with Rishabhanatha, the first tirthankara (supreme

---

[52] Y 52:1-4 (trans. Bartholomae) (https://www.avesta.org/yasna/index.html#y35). Reprinted with permission.

[53] Y 8:5-7 (trans. Mills) (https://www.avesta.org/yasna/index.html#y35). Reprinted with permission.

[54] Y 60:11 (trans. Mills) (https://www.avesta.org/yasna/index.html#y35). Reprinted with permission

[55] Jain, Parveen. *An Introduction to Jain Philosophy* (DK Printworld, 2019, Kindle Edition), pp. 336-7.

preacher) of Jainism in the current time cycle of Jain cosmology. However, Jains consider time to have no beginning and no end, rather occurring in cycles that repeat perpetually. Thus, Jainism is eternal, arising again and again as a means to help human beings gain liberation. A tirthankara means a "ford maker," a being who has conquered samsara and is thus able to help others cross the sea of interminable rebirths and deaths. Rishabhanatha, the first of the twenty-four tirthankaras, is also known as "Lord of the Beginning," as he was the first tirthankara in the current cycle of time, initiating the religion. According to Jain cosmology, he lived millions of years ago.

The one credited with reviving Jainism more recently is Mahavira, who was the 24th Tirthankara. He lived in India about 2500 years ago and was a contemporary with Gautama Buddha. He practiced intense meditation, lived an ascetic life, and taught for over thirty years. He emphasized that true liberation could only be obtained by purifying the inner self, rather than by external rituals. Inner purity was what was required for salvation, not external bathing, even if it were in the Ganges. No ritual should be meaningless according to Mahavira. He was the last Tirthankara to appear in the current time cycle.

Jains teach there are five vows which both ascetics and the common person must observe: ahimsa (non-violence - all life is sanctified), no lying or stealing, abstinence for monks and fidelity for common people, and non-attachment to possessions, with monks owning nothing.

Ahimsa, or non-harm, is the foundation for all spiritual achievements, and self-control is the path. Ahimsa is central to the Jain faith, reflected in their vegetarian and vegan dietary habits to avoid causing harm to any being. The lifestyle of ahimsa and asceticism is important, but some find it hard to implement. Mahatma Gandhi considered Mahavira the greatest authority on ahimsa.[56]

These vows were for the purpose of achieving spiritual peace and a

---

[56] https://www.arihantainstitute.org/blog/25-modern-jainism-defined-belief-history-literature-facts.

better rebirth with the ultimate goal of moksha (liberation) through one's own efforts. Mahivira stressed non-possessiveness and equality, including not causing harm to others by forcing them into any particular caste.

The three "jewels" of Jainism are right faith, right knowledge, and right conduct. When these are achieved, in that order, liberation happens. Accepting the first jewel is needed to progress any further.[57]

The Jain scriptures and texts include the Agamas[58] and the Tattvartha Sutra. Jains are primarily in western India but have also spread to Nepal, the United Kingdom, Kenya, Canada, the United States, Tanzania and other countries.[59]

The following are excerpts from the *Tattvartha Sutra* ("On the Nature of Reality"):

I bow to the Lord, the promulgator of the path to liberation, the destroyer of mountains, of karmas and the knower of the whole of reality, so that I may realize these qualities.

Right faith, right knowledge, and right conduct (together) constitute the path to liberation.

Belief in substances ascertained as they are is right faith.

Charity is the giving of one's wealth to another for mutual benefit.

The consequences of violence etc. are calamity and reproach in this world and in the next.

Vulgar jokes, vulgar jokes accompanied by gesticulation, garrulity, unthinkingly indulging in too much action, keeping too many consumable and non-consumable objects, are the five transgressions of the vow of desisting from unnecessary sin.[60]

---

[57] https://jainpedia.org/themes/principles/jain-beliefs/the-three-gems/.

[58] https://www.jainfoundation.in/JAINLIBRARY/books/agama_023168_hr6.pdf.

[59] https://www.worldatlas.com/articles/countries-with-the-largest-jain-populations.html.

[60] https://archive.org/details/tattvarthbook10webf/page/n13/mode/2up.

HINDUISM[61]

The religion of Hinduism had its beginnings approximately four thousand years ago in the Indus Valley (northwest India and modern-day Pakistan). Prior to being given the comprehensive name of Hinduism, the people would say they practiced the eternal religion known as Sanatana Dharma, which means righteousness that has no beginning and no end.

Hinduism is a mystical religion concerned with achieving oneness with or realization of the Ultimate Reality. This is regarded as achievable, rather than theoretical. Although there are various disciplines (yogas) to pursue the goal under the wider umbrella of Hinduism, each is considered its own real path to realization. However, final liberation and oneness with Reality or God requires grace from the presence of that Ultimate Reality.

Hindu scripture includes both revealed texts (considered non-authored, transmitted from the Divine realm through ancient seers called rishis), including the Vedas and Upanishads, and authored texts, such as the Mahabarata, Ramayana, Sutras, Shastras, Puranas, and others.

The *Chandogya Upanishad* describes what the people of Sanatana Dharma thought about the concepts of God and soul. Some followers of Sanatana Dharma were devoted to an omnipotent god that defies definition and is eternal (Brahman), and consider themselves to be emanations of that God, to which they will return at the time of moksha (salvation), like rivers running into the ocean. Others consider that there is only eternal divine consciousness and we (and the universes) are but divine projections from this cosmic energy. Our mind, will, emotions, and physical bodies are simply faculties by which that divine consciousness enacts the life of the universe—there is no distinct personal self, only that divine consciousness or Self (a.k.a. "Atman") having forgotten its true nature. Realization of this Self, this Oneness of God, or

---

[61] https://www.history.com/topics/religion/hinduism#,
https://www.worldhistory.org/hinduism/.

this cosmic energy/consciousness, is the goal of every human life.

Our essence or soul is eternal, as written in the *Bhagavad Gita*, Chapter 2:[62]

I say to thee weapons reach not the Life;
Flame burns it not, waters cannot o'erwhelm,
Nor dry winds wither it. Impenetrable,
Unentered, unassailed, unharmed, untouched,
Immortal, all-arriving, stable, sure,
Invisible, ineffable, by word
And thought uncompassed, ever all itself,
Thus is the Soul declared!

He who shall think, "Lo! I am slain!" those both
Know naught! Life cannot slay. Life is not slain!
Never the spirit was born; the spirit shall cease to be never;
Never was time it was not; End and Beginning are dreams!
Birthless and deathless and changeless remaineth the spirit forever;
Death hath not touched it at all, dead though the house of it seems!

Considering the eternality of life, soul, and God, Hindus are very respectful of life, including that of all living creatures. Many are vegetarian as they do not want to kill and cook animals. As with Jainism, the principle of ahimsa, non-harm or non-violence, is the guide in life.

Belief in morality and "dharma," which is righteousness or right conduct, are prominent. Through right conduct it is believed the soul will eventually achieve "moksha," or salvation, and oneness with the divine, ending the cycle of rebirths (reincarnation). Karma, the law of cause and effect, guides how the universe unfolds, and is considered to continue between and through each successive life. The symbol for this belief is called the "wheel of righteousness" and is found on the Indian flag; the wheel represents continual motion towards and pursuit of

---

[62] (trans. Arnold).

righteousness which holds up this world and all other worlds.

The path of right conduct leading to moksha is called yoga, which means "union," and in practical terms refers to a practice that facilitates awareness of the Self and, ultimately, adherence in an ecstatic, blissful awareness called samadhi. Yoga is both a science and a discipline, meant to free the practitioner from ensnarement in worldly concerns and lead them to freedom. Karma yoga is the yoga of right action, involving selfless and loving service to others without attachment.

Find full reward
Of doing right in right! Let right deeds be
Thy motive, not the fruit which comes from them.
And live in action![63]

Bhakti yoga is the path of love and devotion, Jnana yoga is the path of wisdom, and Raja yoga is the path of meditation. Hatha yoga concerns itself with purifying the body by way of breathing techniques and body postures (asanas) and is a facilitator of meditation. The Western world has popularized hatha yoga and some Westerners practice this as a form of exercise for the physical body, as well as a form of meditation for mental calmness. This is different from their original purpose. Westerners can still use this method in their own spiritual pursuit when combined with the other types of yoga.

Throughout the Hindu scriptures are stories of messengers or saviors, called "Avatars," who came into earthly life at times of great wickedness to reset human righteousness in society. According to the *Srimad-Bhagavatam*, there is one remaining avatar, Kalki, who is expected to arrive riding on a white horse with a sword to eradicate the wicked and reestablish righteous human society. Some believe he will not return for another 427,000 years, while others believe his arrival is not too far away—it depends on how one starts the counting of time!

In the *Mahabharata*, the Harivamsha, and the Bhagavata-purana,

---

[63] BG 2:47 (trans. Arnold).

you can read of the embodiment of the Supreme Person of the Godhead in the form of Lord Krishna.

The *Bhagavad Gita* is the story of a conversation between Lord Krishna and Arjuna, a warrior going into a pivotal battle about which he is conflicted. Arjuna seeks insight and guidance from Krishna and what follows is a conversation for the ages. In Chapter 8 of the *Bhagavad Gita*, Krishna says:

I BRAHMA am! the One Eternal GOD,
And ADHYATMAN is My Being's name,
The Soul of Souls! What goeth forth from Me,
Causing all life to live, is KARMA called:
And, Manifested in divided forms,
I am the ADHIBHUTA, Lord of Lives;
And ADHIDAIVA, Lord of all the Gods,
Because I am PURUSHA, who begets.
And ADHIYAJNA, Lord of Sacrifice,
I—speaking with thee in this body here—
Am, thou embodied one! (for all the shrines
Flame unto Me!)
With never-wavering will of firmest faith,
Owning none other Gods: all come to Me,
The Uttermost, Purusha, Holiest![64]

Lord Krishna also gives insight and direction for the time of impending death, emphasizing the importance of being in a state of worship at this time and especially repeating the word "Om," as this is the primordial sound or word spoken at creation.

And, at the hour of death,
He that hath meditated Me alone,
In putting off his flesh, comes forth to Me,
Enters into My Being--doubt thou not!

---

[64] (trans. Arnold) https://www.gutenberg.org/files/2388/2388-h/2388-h.htm#chap08.

But, if he meditated otherwise
At hour of death, in putting off the flesh,
He goes to what he looked for, Kunti's Son!
Because the Soul is fashioned to its like.
Have Me, then, in thy heart always! and fight!
Thou too, when heart and mind are fixed on Me,
Shalt surely come to Me!
Who cleave, who seek in Me
Refuge from birth and death, those have the Truth!
Those know Me BRAHMA; know Me Soul of Souls,
The ADHYATMAN; know KARMA, my work;
Know I am ADHIBHUTA, Lord of Life,
And ADHIDAIVA, Lord of all the Gods,
And ADHIYAJNA, Lord of Sacrifice;
Worship Me well, with hearts of love and faith,
And find and hold me in the hour of death. [65]
I am, of all this boundless Universe-
The Father, Mother, Ancestor, and Guard!
The end of Learning! That which purifies
In lustral water! I am OM![66]
As the infinite (Brahman) alone.
Om Peace! Peace! Peace![67]

Hinduism has survived for thousands of years and is now spread over the globe, especially via the Indian diaspora. With no singular founder or prophet, nor an overarching governing board, Hinduism remains one of the most diverse religions in the world.

SIKHISM[68]

One day in the Punjab region of India, about five to six hundred years

---

[65] Ibid.

[66] BG 9 (trans. Arnold).

[67] Shanti Mantra from the Isha and Brihadaranyaka Upanishad.

[68] https://www.britannica.com/topic/Sikhism.

ago, a young Hindu man, Nanak Bedi, and his Muslim musician friend, Mardana, went for a dip in the river. In his early thirties at this time, Nanak had always been a very inward and spiritual man, and he had both Hindu and Muslim friends.

After some time in the river, Mardana noticed he had not seen the return of Nanak, though his clothes were still on the riverbank. He frantically called the townspeople to help him look for his friend but with no success, so they sadly decided he must have drowned. Three days later he appeared on the riverbank still wet from his dip, his face shining. He said he had been continuously in the Heavenly realm and was given the knowledge that: "There is no Hindu; there is no Musalman (Muslim)." Nanak became an ascetic and a prolific poet, writing of the wondrous experience in the Divine Realm that he had. He began to spread his message that there is only one God. Rather than promoting what he called meaningless rituals, he emphasized meditation on the one Creator God. He wrote:

Guru Nanak believed that dressing like an ascetic did not make you one but rather treating everyone alike and remaining pure in your thoughts and your life while living in an impure world.[69]

Nanak preached his message amongst the common people, no matter whether they were Hindu, Muslim, or any other faith, expounding on the brotherhood of all people as the creation of the One God. Guru Nanak promoted faith in and meditation toward the Creator God to whom we all have equal access, toward the divine unity and equality of all humankind and toward the pursuit of service and justice.

Over time, Sikh traditions developed. The men are known for not cutting their hair as an expression of honor to God by keeping what God has given, symbolized by the hair. To keep the hair orderly, they wear a turban. This also identifies them as a Sikh, although this is not considered necessary for Moksha (salvation).

Nanak's poetry and teachings were collected and compiled in the *Guru Granth Sahib*, which also includes teachings by five other Sikh

---

[69] Guru Granth Sahib, Suhi (https://www.sikhheritagegroup.com/the-sikh-gurus.html).

gurus, as well as teachings by some Hindu saints and one Muslim saint. Sikhs, as well as Jews and Christians, are known for their use of the bridal paradigm, symbolizing oneness and intimacy with the Creator. The compositions in *Guru Granth Sahib* are rendered poetically and set to classical north Indian music, or ragas. Guru Nanak was the faith's first guru, followed by nine subsequent gurus, the last one declaring that the scriptures themselves were to be the eternally living successor.

Many Muslims in India regard Guru Nanak as a Sufi Muslim due to the overlapping of some of their beliefs, particularly that there is one God who is formless. However, Sikhism believes that no one religion contains all truth and, therefore, Sikhs do not emphasize proselytizing.

There is a significant history of religious persecution of Sikhs in India, so Sikhs developed a strong sense of self defense and, in 1699, an order was created called the Khalsa, tasked with protecting freedom of religion. The writings of the *Karni Nama* and *Raj Nama*, books of Sikh prophecy, tell of the future return of a strong Guru to lead the world to peace, but these writings are considered controversial amongst some Sikhs.[70]

Nanak wrote many hymns praising the One Universal Creator God. He refers to dancing for the love of God and sees believers as spiritual brides in love with their Creator Husband/Lord merging into the light of God.

Following are some excerpts of hymns from the *Guru Granth Sahib*:[71]

"O! my friends, the Master will call,

the poor swan (life) will leave, body shall become a heap of dust."

One (God) is formless, dynamic. True is (His) name. (He is the) Person who creates. (He is) beyond fear and animosity (all love). (He is) eternal Being. (He is) not subject to birth and death. (He is) self existent. (He is) realized by the grace of Guru.

You are a supreme king, I call you a chief, how it fits in your glory.

---

[70] https://archive.org/details/KarniNama/Karni%20Nama%20%282%29/mode/2up?view=theater.

[71] https://archive.org/details/darshan_singh/darshan_singh/page/1680/mode/2up public domain

Whatever you give, I speak O! my Master, I, the foolish, cannot say anything else.

Help me to know, I will sing your attributes,
like to live in truth by your will.
Whatever is created, is by you, it is all your love.
I do not know your limits, O! my Master, I, the blind, have no wisdom.
What to relate (about you), when I try to relate, I find that unrelatable cannot be related.
I will relate what you like me to relate, even that shall be little about your greatness.
One word is living in my being, I need not to take birth again.
O! my mother, the Merciful has pierced my mind, (with the arrow of love)
who knows other's (mine) pain?
I do not care for anyone (other than God).
The inaccessible, the unknowable, the uncountable, the infinite Master, please take care of me.
You are pervading in waters, in lands, in nether regions, in every body the light is yours. The education, wisdom, intellect all are yours, the shade (protection) is also of your home.
All living beings are in your refuge, you are to care for all.
You yourself are a word and you are the flag,
You are a knower and you are known.
Your create and creating you see your might.
You are the giver, remembering your name is accepted.
Such is your name, O! divine God.
If name is blessed, light illuminates the darkness.
After tasting, I left (the worldliness), so now there is no doubt.
Once father is seen (there), (the child) never becomes illegitimate.
When in union, there is no fear.
The Creator does and He gets it done.
By the word of Guru, the mind concentrates, in ease.
Enjoying the love of God, mind is obedient.

Why should we live without God? realize Him through the word.

O! mother, how can I live without seeing Him.

Without God, my heart lives not for a while.

If I forget my Master, I will die in agony.

Nanak says, "God's name is my capital, my wealth."

God is one, realized by the grace of true Guru.

Useless is the food, useless is the sleep, useless is the dress, that is worn.

Useless is body, the family, in whose company, I could not meet my Master.

Those, who forgot the feet (service) of God, and are in the love of the other, are not allowed to be intuned with Him.

O! God, the giver of life, all the people are your servants, you cast their sorrows away.

Only that person is liberated who is intuned with One. He is ever in the company of God."

BUDDHISM (OR BUDDHA DHARMA)[72]

About 2500 years ago, there was a prince born in the Indian subcontinent in an area now considered modern-day Nepal. His name was Siddhartha Gautama. He left the family palace one day and discovered so much suffering that he was moved to leave home, give up his titles and wealth, and seek enlightenment. Gautama traveled to a place now known as Bodh Gaya in modern day northeastern India where he sat under a bodhi tree and began to meditate, refusing to get up until he had attained enlightenment. He continued in intense meditation for forty-nine days, received enlightenment and began to teach those around him what he had learned. About two hundred years after his death, he became known as "the Buddha," or the "enlightened one," and the religion became known as Buddha Dharma (doctrine of the enlightened one), or in modern English, Buddhism. He called his teachings the "Four Noble Truths" and the "Eightfold Path."[73]

---

[72] https://www.britannica.com/topic/Buddhism.

[73] https://education.nationalgeographic.org/resource/buddhism/.

The Four Noble Truths describe that there is suffering (dukkha) in life and that the cause of this suffering is desire (samudaya); therefore, to end suffering one must end desire (nirodha) by way of self-control, a moderate lifestyle, and detachment (magga). This path for ending suffering became known as the Middle Way, as it refrained from both extremes of asceticism and a life based on the sole pursuit of earthly, sensual pleasures. The definition of dukkha is difficult to translate but can be likened to chronic dissonance or an unsatisfactory experience resulting from the expectation of happiness.

Eventually, the Middle Way was called the Eightfold Path, specifying eight practices to achieve liberation from suffering: Right Belief, Right Thinking, Right Speech, Right Conduct, Right Livelihood, Right Effort, Right Mindfulness and Right Meditation. These practices and insights about liberation are considered the same as liberation itself.

Gautama taught that the "cause of human misery is ignorance," and the remedy is to dispel ignorance.[74] By ignorance he was referring to humans prizing what is not worth prizing—for example, grieving when we shouldn't or spending our life in pursuit of worthless objects. Rather, we should live life focused on ensuring the greatest happiness for our fellow human beings and ourselves—and the least suffering. This dispelling of ignorance is accomplished by implementing the Four Noble Truths. By becoming detached we can conquer this thirst for the pleasures of life, which brings sorrow. The person who applies these teachings will achieve Nirvana (or freedom from continual rebirths). Nirvana, or salvation, is absence of desire, so one is then at rest.[75]

The Buddha's teachings were especially attractive to the poor and marginalized in his society because of the difficulty of complex Hindu rituals, which required a priestly caste, and which entrenched the caste system. Buddha's teaching was by contrast much simpler and more accessible, as he taught the equality of all. However, though the teaching may have appeared simple, in order to gain the knowledge to

---

[74] https://www.gutenberg.org/files/30216/30216-h/30216-h.htm#chap02.

[75] https://www.gutenberg.org/files/30216/30216-h/30216-h.htm#chap04.

implement the Four Noble Truths and Eightfold Path, it required much effort and time for meditation and study.

The Buddha taught that there is no fixed human soul, though he was not a nihilist. He explained that we do not have a permanent essence that we can say is "me" or "mine"; we are simply reborn countless times in our pursuit of nirvana, retaining karma from prior lives. He did not encourage the idea of a Creator God, as he considered such questions fruitless and not fundamental to following the Eightfold Path or achieving Nirvana. He stressed instead the importance of living in the moment.

Body is not self, feelings are not self, perception is not self, mental constructs are not self and consciousness is not self... When one sees this one becomes detached from these things, being detached the passions fade, when the passions have faded one is free, and being free one knows one is free.[76]

While Buddhism began in India, it spread to different parts of the world, evolving in each region a bit differently. This was in large part due to an Indian Emperor known as Ashoka, who lived two hundred years after the historical Buddha and became a great champion of Buddha's teachings. He built many Buddhist monasteries and helped Buddha's teachings spread from India northward to Tibet, over to China, and throughout Asia. Thus, in China, Buddhism mingled with indigenous Taoism and Confucianism; in Japan, a branch of Chinese Buddhism called Chan Buddhism became Zen Buddhism; in India and Tibet, Buddhism mingled with tantrism and the Tibetan Bon tradition; and in Southeast Asia, Theravada Buddhism grew.

In this process of migration and assimilation, three specific expressions or traditions of the Buddhist teachings developed. The first, the Sravakayana, which is considered the oldest, is mostly associated with Theravada Buddhism, and emphasizes individual liberation. The second is the Mahayana, which developed later, heavily influenced Zen Buddhism, Pure Land Buddhism, and Tibetan Buddhism, and emphasizes the importance of helping to liberate all sentient beings. And

[76] Samyutta Nikaya 1884

finally, there is the Vajrayana, a highly ritualized version of Buddhism that includes the use of visualization, mantra recitation, tantra, and other practices, and that informed much of Tibetan Buddhism and various esoteric schools.[77]

All traditions of Buddhism share the Four Noble Truths and emphasize the importance of the "Three Jewels": the Buddha, the Dharma, and the Sangha.[78] This means revering Buddha (which may include many other buddhas besides Siddhartha Gautama); practicing the Dharma, meaning implementing the universal truths taught in the Four Noble Truths and the Eightfold Path; and cultivating the Sangha, or community of Buddhist practitioners, monks and nuns who carry out the teachings of the Buddha and are sustained by the lay people who gain merit from supporting them.

In Theravada Buddhism, practiced in Sri Lanka, Cambodia, Thailand, Laos and Burma/Myanmar, the scriptural canon is called the "Three Baskets." The first part, the Vinaya, is related to issues of morality and recommendations for the orders of monks. The second part, the Suttas, are the teachings of the Buddha. And the third part, the Abhidharma, explains the teachings of the Buddha, including the twenty-four transcendental laws explaining Nature, as well as teachings on the difference between conventional truth and ultimate truth. The teachings of the Buddha are many, but the most important tenet is lovingkindness.

Other popular Buddhist texts include the Dhammapada, the *Lotus Sutra,* the *Heart Sutra* and the *Diamond Sutra.*

The following are some excerpts from Buddhist scriptures and teachings:

The Path:

273. The best of ways is the eightfold; the best of truths the four words; the best of virtues passionlessness; the best of men he who has eyes to see.

---

[77] https://www.lionsroar.com/buddhism/three-yanas/.

[78] https://thebuddhistcentre.com/text/three-jewels.

274. This is the way, there is no other that leads to the purifying of intelligence. Go on this way! Everything else is the deceit of Mara (the tempter).[79]

The Wise Man (Pandita):

76. If you see an intelligent man who tells you where true treasures are to be found, who shows what is to be avoided, and administers reproofs, follow that wise man; it will be better, not worse, for those who follow him.

77. Let him admonish, let him teach, let him forbid what is improper!— he will be beloved of the good, by the bad he will be hated.

78. Do not have evil-doers for friends, do not have low people for friends: have virtuous people for friends, have for friends the best of men.

85. Few are there among men who arrive at the other shore (become Arhats); the other people here run up and down the shore.

86. But those who, when the law has been well preached to them, follow the law, will pass across the dominion of death, however difficult to overcome.

87, 88. A wise man should leave the dark state (of ordinary life), and follow the bright state (of the Bhikshu). After going from his home to a homeless state, he should in his retirement look for enjoyment where there seemed to be no enjoyment. Leaving all pleasures behind, and calling nothing his own, the wise man should purge himself from all the troubles of the mind.

89. Those whose mind is well grounded in the (seven) elements of knowledge, who without clinging to anything, rejoice in freedom from attachment, whose appetites have been conquered, and who are full of light, are free (even) in this world.[80]

The *Heart Sutra:*

---

[79] Dhammapada Chapter 20, The Way.

[80] Dhammapada Chapter 6, The Wise Man.

The Bodhisattva Avalokitesvara,

Whilst in profound Prajna Paramita,

Saw illume the void of the five skandhas And prevailed over all pain and peril.

Sariputta, image and void differ not, Image is void and void is image.

So too sense and thought,

Conduct and Consciousness.

Sariputta, the manifold dharmas Are void and neither arise nor cease,

Are neither defiled nor pure and neither Swell nor dwindle.

Thus, voidness has no image; no sense. Thought, conduct and consciousness. Without eyes, ears, nose, tongue, body or mind; Without sight and sound, or scent, taste, Feelings of touch, and dharma.

With no realm of vision or realm of awareness. Neither dullness nor the end of dullness. Neither decline and demise Nor the end of decline and demise. Devoid of pain, its causes, and need to cease it, Without wisdom or gain And with nothing to attain.

Bodhisattvas with Prajna Paramita Have easeful hearts free from fear. Forfeiting minds of mirage like dreams, They achieve ultimate Nibbana.

Hence, know that Prajna Paramita Is the greatly divine mantra.

The most luminous mantra,

The unsurpassed mantra.

And the peerless mantra.

Able to banish all misery;

Forever true and never false!

Thus, proclaim the Prajna Paramita Mantra, And chant it so:

Jie di jie di bo luo jie di bo luo seng jie di pu ti sa po he

The Buddhas that were, are now, and yet to come Shall all through Prajna Paramita achieve Anuttara- samyak- sambodhi.[81]

Milarepa was a Tibetan Buddhist who had once been a murderer, then found liberation in meditation and emphasized that this practice is pivotal. He believed that no matter what the rest of the world is doing, one must devotedly seek the Truth in meditation so that you live out of loving-kindness and all your works for others come out of this foundation of loving-kindness.[82]

TAOISM[83]

China was the cradle for Taoism, Buddhism and Confucianism. All these religions and/or philosophies have been of major global significance due to their profound effects on how humanity deals with the unknowable, the unfixable, and the need for love and compassion.

The story of Chinese mysticism goes back thousands of years. About five to seven thousand years ago in China, there were people who worshipped a Supreme God as well as lesser gods, according to archeologic findings.[84] Most religious and philosophical traditions in China (as elsewhere in the world) were passed down orally. Then, about 2400 years ago, an anonymously written book appeared called the *Neiye (The Study of Inner Cultivation)*, which details practical wisdom for meditation and working on one's inner self.

Among the mystics of Taoism, Lao Tzu is perhaps the most well known in the West as the author of the classical Taoist text the *Tao Te Ching*.[85] He was a contemporary of Confucius and lived and worked as

---

[81] The Heart Sutra (https://archive.org/details/heartsutra2018?source=post_page-----d26e07c7241e---------------------------------) page 8.

[82] https://encyclopediaofbuddhism.org/wiki/Milarepa.

[83] Daoism and Taoism are interchangeable terms. Daoism is closer to the Chinese pronunciation, but the term Taoism is more traditional.

[84] https://www.worldhistory.org/article/891/religion-in-ancient-china/.

[85] Also spelled Dao De Jing.

a scholar and teacher. The legend of Lao Tzu says that after he began to cultivate the Way (the Tao) and could no longer tolerate the decadent society in which he lived, he rode out of town on an ox but wrote down the *Tao Te Ching* before he left. This book remains the cornerstone of Taoist writings. Lao Tzu is more correctly said to be a cultivator of Taoism, rather than its founder.[86]

Lao Tzu was thought to be older than Confucius, who consulted him from time to time about ritual protocols. Another foundational Taoist text, the *Chuang Tzu*, relates the story of one of their meetings:

> *On returning from this visit to Lao Tzŭ, Confucius did not speak for three days. A disciple asked him, saying, "Master, when you saw Lao Tzŭ, in what direction did you admonish him?" "I saw a Dragon," replied Confucius, "—a Dragon which by convergence showed a body, by radiation became colour, and riding upon the clouds of Heaven, nourished the two Principles of Creation. My mouth was agape: I could not shut it. How then do you think I was going to admonish Lao Tzŭ?"*[87]

Taoism became more religiously organized about 600 years later when Zhang Daoling,[88] who had studied the *Tao Te Ching*, announced that Lao Tzu appeared to him in a vision and told him the world was coming to an end. He told the people to be prepared as they would become the seed of a new movement of peace. Zhang became the initiator of the lineage of Celestial Masters to promote this movement.

What followed was a very long series of political wars and persecutions of Taoists. Consequently, the Taoist leaders and priests were virtually eliminated by being forced into labor camps or leaving the country. This had the indirect consequence of the global spread of Taoism. Out of Taoism came the concepts of Yin and Yang, the practice

---

[86] https://education.nationalgeographic.org/resource/taoism/.

[87] Chuang Tzu, Chapter 14 (https://www.gutenberg.org/cache/epub/59709/pg59709-images.html#Page_56).

[88] https://www.britannica.com/biography/Zhang-Daoling.

of acupuncture, and Tai Chi and Qi Gong, which helped to spread the underlying beliefs of Taoism in the West.

The Tao is the inner and natural way that is within and all around us, spontaneously giving rise to all that is. Its most noteworthy characteristic is the balance between the complementary polarities of yin and yang.[89] This spontaneous, harmonious unfolding of the universe can be described as flow, or ziran, which is a pivotal concept in Taoism.

The practice of "wu wei" or action by non-action, is a means of coming into right relationship with the Tao, like water flowing. Such effortless action or harmony with the universe allows one to become free by letting go of selfish desires and appreciating simplicity. This requires recognizing one's interdependence with others and the universe.

Thus, the primary goal of Taoism is union with the Tao and being in harmony with the flow of the Tao (ziran). Lao Tzu is considered the incarnation of one of the "Three Pure Ones," and he is worshipped in Taoism along with other Celestial Masters. The most important virtues in Taoism are the Three Jewels (similar to Buddhism):

The most important virtues in Taoism are the Three Jewels (similar to Buddhism): compassion, moderation and humility. The following are excerpts from the *Tao Te Ching*:

PART 1.

Ch. 1.1. The Tao that can be trodden is not the enduring and unchanging Tao. The name that can be named is not the enduring and unchanging name.

2. (Conceived of as) having no name, it is the Originator of heaven and earth; (conceived of as) having a name, it is the Mother of all things.

3. Always without desire we must be found,

---

89 https://www.britannica.com/topic/dao.

If its deep mystery we would sound;

But if desire always within us be,

Its outer fringe is all that we shall see.

4. Under these two aspects, it is really the same; but as development takes place, it receives the different names. Together we call them the Mystery. Where the Mystery is the deepest is the gate of all that is subtle and wonderful.

2.1. All in the world know the beauty of the beautiful, and in doing this they have (the idea of) what ugliness is; they all know the skill of the skilful, and in doing this they have (the idea of) what the want of skill is.

2. So it is that existence and non-existence give birth the one to (the idea of) the other; that difficulty and ease produce the one (the idea of) the other; that length and shortness fashion out the one the figure of the other; that (the ideas of) height and lowness arise from the contrast of the one with the other; that the musical notes and tones become harmonious through the relation of one with another; and that being before and behind give the idea of one following another.

3. Therefore the sage manages affairs without doing anything, and conveys his instructions without the use of speech.

4. All things spring up, and there is not one which declines to show itself; they grow, and there is no claim made for their ownership; they go through their processes, and there is no expectation (of a reward for the results). The work is accomplished, and there is no resting in it (as an achievement).

The work is done, but how no one can see;

'Tis this that makes the power not cease to be.

...

4.1. The Tao is (like) the emptiness of a vessel; and in our employment of it we must be on our guard against all fulness. How deep and unfathomable it is, as if it were the Honoured Ancestor of all things!

2. We should blunt our sharp points, and unravel the complications of things; we should attemper our brightness, and bring ourselves into agreement with the obscurity of others. How pure and still the Tao is, as if it would ever so continue!

...

7.1. Heaven is long-enduring and earth continues long. The reason why heaven and earth are able to endure and continue thus long is because they do not live of, or for, themselves. This is how they are able to continue and endure.[90]

CONFUCIANISM[91]

Kong Qiu was born about 2500 years ago in a coastal province of Eastern China, now known as Shandong. His father died when he was three years old, and he was raised by his mother in poverty. He became an educator in his 30s and an advocate for public welfare. Kong Qui ultimately became known as Kong Fuzi (meaning Master Kong) which was latinized to "Confucius" by Jesuit Missionaries in China. Confucius was known for his humility and was quoted as saying: "Even when walking in a party of no more than three I can always be certain of learning from those I am with. There will be good qualities that I can select for imitation and bad ones that will teach me what requires correction in myself."[92]

His modesty and scholarliness produced a large following. His students ultimately wrote down his sayings in a book known as *The Analects of Confucius.*

Confucius was a contemporary of Siddhartha Gautama (the Buddha), Pythagoras, and Lao Tzu. Some people do not consider Confucianism a religion but rather a philosophy. Confucius did educate his students on worship of ancestors and the proper method of rituals,

---

[90] https://www.gutenberg.org/cache/epub/216/pg216-images.html.

[91] https://education.nationalgeographic.org/resource/confucianism/;
https://www.britannica.com/topic/Confucianism.

[92] Analects 7: 21.

as it was his belief that proper attention to rituals had a stabilizing effect on society. And he did refer to the spiritual realm from time to time:

Since the death of King Wen [founder of the Zhou dynasty] does not the mission of culture (wen) rest here in me? If Heaven intends this culture to be destroyed, those who come after me will not be able to have any part of it. If Heaven does not intend this culture to be destroyed, then what can the men of Kuang do to me?[93]

The idea of "filial piety" was key to his teachings and his writings always provided a guide to his students for family life and life in society. *The Analects of Confucius* continues to provide a philosophical and cultural undergirding for a stable society throughout China and much of Asia. Though he called himself a "transmitter who invented nothing," his philosophy of harmonious societal relationships, personal morals, and a ruler's responsibility to lead by virtuous example contributed greatly to the stability of his society. This philosophy also spread onward to Singapore, Taiwan, Japan, Vietnam and Korea. Devotion to "filial piety" (family) is evident in all these cultures to this day and is considered the strength behind stability in the societies and governments of these nations.

He promoted a sort of reverse of the "Golden Rule," that is to say, *Don't do to others what you don't want done to you.* He also wrote poetry and was a proponent of music, as it helped to elevate societal rituals, develop morals, and refine the intellect of individuals and families and, by extension, society:

My children, why do you not study the Book of Poetry? The Odes serve to stimulate the mind. They may be used for purposes of self-contemplation. They teach the art of sociability. They show how to regulate feelings of resentment. From them you learn the more immediate duty of serving one's father, and the remoter one of serving one's prince.[94]

Confucius also taught his students the importance of recognizing

---

[93] Analects 9: 5.

[94] Analects 17.

the ordinances of Heaven, trustworthiness and sincerity as the foundation for all other virtues. He taught this should be carried through from the individual to the family then to society.

CHAP III. 1. The Master said, 'Without recognising the ordinances of Heaven, it is impossible to be a superior man. 2. 'Without an acquaintance with the rules of Propriety, it is impossible for the character to be established. 3. 'Without knowing the force of words, it is impossible to know men. [95]

2500 years after Confucius, you can still see the profound effect of his teachings that virtue should be developed in the individual, the family, and the administrators of society, and that all should be held accountable. There is no society that could not benefit from Confucius' practical teachings of virtue and wisdom.

SHINTOISM[96]

Shintoism developed in Japan over two thousand years ago and is generally considered an indigenous religion in Japan. The word Shinto means "the Way of the gods" or "the Way of the Kami" (divine power or beings or spiritual forces), and this word was used to distinguish it from Buddhism, which was growing in Japan at that time as well. There is no apparent founder nor dogmas, but it remains faithfully practiced in Japan and by its followers all over the world. There are two main relevant books, the *Kojiki* and *Nihongi*, which are compilations of myths, legends, and teachings previously passed down orally. The *Yengishiki* contains specific directions for the ceremonies and offerings used in Shinto worship.[97]

Shintoism is practiced alongside Buddhism in Japan, as its beliefs and practices, like those of Buddhism, do not claim to be exclusive. Early Shinto was very appreciative of life, birth, and, naturally, it had

---

[95] Analects II and III.

[96] https://www.britannica.com/topic/Shinto.

[97] https://www.britannica.com/topic/shinten.

an open attitude towards women. Rituals are important to the practice and are a portal to the Divine realm, allowing interface with the kami. Purity is emphasized as well as respect for family, subordination of the individual before the group, and the joy that comes from harmony.

This harmony is especially appreciated in nature, to which great reverence is given. Shinto has a very positive and optimistic approach to life and prefers not to place too much emphasis on sin and its effects, as this is believed to produce melancholy.

Shintoism today emphasizes reverence for the Divine and remains strong and persistent despite its many evolutions over thousands of years. What Shinto gives us is stillness, and its ceremonies help you feel the calm and sacredness of nature, like the very subtle awareness of fall in the air. Some words are so sacred that they can only be heard in this stillness and quietness. The Tea Ceremony has long been a spiritual experience during which beauty and nobility in nature is contemplated in silence.

Cultural identity is a very powerful influence in Japanese society and the practice of Shintoism has a unifying effect on the culture, creating strong bonds. The rituals, music, and art in Shintoism are beautiful, enhance the experience of the Divine and have been a primary vehicle for passing this religion down through the centuries.

Though Shinto is not usually portrayed as a monotheistic religion, many give honor to the "god of all Kami" when praying. The meaning of the term does not imply plurality and is simply the divine essence that gives rise to all things. There is a very poetic tendency in this Japanese religion.

The following excerpt is from an early 20th century history and commentary on Japanese culture:

"When Heaven and Earth were in a state of chaos, there was first of all a deity, whose name was Umashi-ashi-kabi-hiko-ji no Mikoto. Next there was Kuni-soko-tachi no Mikoto."

Uniquely, there are mirrors at some shrines for gazing at one's reflection while thinking on the divine: *"In Kojiki we read:*

"The mirror typifies the human heart, which, when perfectly placid

and clear, reflects the very image of the deity. "Think of heavenly things, to stifle passion and all evil thought, so that the disc should reveal a pure and lovely soul."

"Again, we see the quietness and stillness, which promotes introspection and calm and a sense of sacredness in Shinto spirituality in the Tea Ceremony. Those who seek a spiritual experience when attending a Tea Ceremony: "drank their tea and meditated and went forth into the world again better and stronger for having contemplated in silence the beautiful and the noble in religion, art and nature. Seeking always to be in harmony with the great rhythm of the universe, they were ever prepared to enter the unknown."[98]

TENRIKYO[99]

Tenrikyo is another important religion of the world. It was founded in Japan by a woman named Nakayama Miki, born in 1798. Though in her early life she followed the principles of both Shintoism and Buddhism, a common practice in Japan, she had a life-changing experience in 1838 while she was praying for healing of her family members. She became possessed by what she called "God-the-Parent," and what followed were many years of serial revelations that she wrote about. Nakayama writes that she became indwelt by God-the-Parent and, in effect, became a shrine of the One God. She was meant to inform humans of their origins, purpose, and means of salvation as she began a life of austerity. She wrote down her teachings and composed music for worship in what is called the *Ofudesaki* text (the English name is the *Tip of the Writing Brush*).

This religion is not a sect of Shintoism nor Buddhism but rather an independent religion that started with this particular event in Nakayama's life. Tenrikyo originally had to be registered in Japan as a

---

[98] Davis, F. Hadland, *The Myths and Legends of Japan* (London: 1912) page 296. (https://archive.org/details/mythslegendsofja00davi)

[99] https://www.tenrikyo.or.jp/eng/history/.

sect of Shintoism due to government regulations at that time. There are some commonalities with Shintoism but not substantial ones. Especially of note is that the religion of Tenrikyo does not share the books of *Kojiki* and *Nihon-gi* from Shintoism.

What was revealed to Nakayama Miki at the time she was possessed by God-the-Parent is that one single God created the entire universe and humankind and is named Tenri-O-no-Mikoto. The purpose of the creation of humankind is to have a joyous life, and each one is given a body for that experience. Nakayama wrote that the body is "a thing lent and a thing borrowed" for this lifetime. Our mind is our own, but our body is lent to us by God-the-Parent. Our mind is the territory we choose to submit to God-the-Parent in prayer.

In Tenrikyo one must not be selfish but put others first. Daily prayer is to "sweep away the dust from the mind," especially selfishness and pride. The relationship between God-the-Parent and humans is mutually loving and grows to a more intimate relationship with ongoing prayer and service. God-the-Parent is a personal god and wants to guide humans and share in their joy. The joyous life will ultimately include all of humanity. Practicing life in prayer, we learn to accept every event with a positive attitude and gratitude, even when suffering.

God-the-Parent guided all religions. Other gods, created by God-the-Parent, are divine instruments. The goal of Tenrikyo members is to make God-the-Parent known and to perform acts of service to promote the Joyous Life. As a result, members of this religion are known in Japan, and the world over, for helping others in times of disaster. They have constructed hospitals and universities as well as orphanages, promising to love the children of others as their own.

The attributes of God-the-Parent are immanence, omnipotence, omniscience, personhood, and transcendence, as well as being a healer for the ones who have faith and a desire to purify their heart.

Tenrikyo has spread all over the world, and there are now centers in Mexico, Argentina, Colombia, Brazil, China, Taiwan, Australia, the Philippines, Thailand, Canada, the USA, France and the United Kingdom.

The following lines are from the Mikagura-uta, Songs for the Service (of Tenrikyo):

Looking all over the world and through all ages,
I find no one who has understood My heart.
So should it be, for I have never taught it before,
It is natural that you know nothing.
This time I, God, revealing Myself to the fore,
teach you all the truth in detail.
You are calling this place the Jiba,
the home of God, in Yamato;
But you do not know of its origin.
If you are told of this origin in full,
Great yearning will come over you, whoever you may be.
If you wish to hear and will come to Me,
I will tell you the truth that this place is the origin of any and
everything.
When I, God, reveal Myself and teach you everything in detail,
all people in the world will become cheerful.
As I hasten to save all of you equally,
I will set out to cheer up all the minds of the world.[100]

SUMMARY – WORDS ON THE WORD TO THE WORLD

If you look at the original writings and original practices from all these religions, you can see that in each one, Eternal Truths are revered. Distortions and conflicts have occurred over time, in part because followers of all religions have not always been diligent in maintaining prayer and meditation and following the Truths set forth. Deviation into selfishness and pride has caused many a downfall. To clearly see the essence of Truth, we must set aside all the human weaknesses that resulted from these downfalls and look instead to the original writings

---

[100] https://archive.org/details/mikagura-uta-the-songs-for-the-service./page/4/mode/2up.

and founders of these faiths. What you also see globally and historically are patterns of both simultaneous revelations as well as progressive revelations. As a loving parent gradually reveals levels of truth to a child as it is growing, you can see similar patterns evolving within religions; foundations were built to withstand the weight of subsequent revelations, leading people into greater intimacy with God.

Wrong perceptions, misinformation, or even ignorance about one's own faith may hamper oneness. These very "Words to the World" hold keys to oneness. For example, many believe certain faiths practice idolatry when, in fact, a physical object may just be a focal point for prayer and not actually worshipped. So, given that none of us are perfect, doesn't it behoove us to humbly listen to and help one another? This will clear the path to oneness of humanity, allowing us to see the True One God so that we can worship in oneness with love—the mission of this book.

If I have seemed disrespectful of God or anyone's faith, please forgive me; I am on this journey, too, and many things remain a mystery to me. I write these words only to fulfill the mandate given to me by the Voice—to promote and bring peace and joy through the oneness of humanity, worshipping the One God in oneness with love. This is an amazing journey I wanted to share as I have been told by many that they, too, believe in the oneness of humanity and One True God. And yet many of these believers find themselves distressed, and they may have even suffered physical injury themselves from the effect of violence and bloodshed in the name of God or religion. I have faithfully reported my spiritual experiences as they occurred, but if I have been wrong about some of my conclusions, I ask forgiveness from True God and from you. I will continue my growth and pursuit of Truth and True God, as I am sure you will too.

Not every aspect of every religion is right, and many human-made religious practices grieve the True One God.

Again, I want to reiterate that the above summaries from the various religions are a result of my conversations with friends and acquaintances over many years and their recommended reading as well as from divinely appointed meetings and spiritual encounters. Not every member of each of these religions will agree with these summaries. This is simply meant as an introduction—sort of like when you meet someone interesting at a party and you want to get to know them further.

Now that we have seen into the future, we can no longer stay where we are. It is Love that picks us up in one place and leaves us in another. I believe that in this book you will find the path to the Love that has overcome obstacles to oneness, peace and joy.

CHAPTER 3

Spirit Words: The Voice through the Hearts of People

PRAYERS AND PASSAGES

ON PRAYER AND MEDITATION

I continuously ask the Voice to guide me on how to pray, what to pray, and who to pray for according to the will of God and the purpose for my life.

Prayerful meditation (a.k.a. contemplative prayer, mental prayer, meditation, mystical union or entering the inner realm) gives you a starting point because it helps you to know where you are. Just as when you use a map, if you do not know where you are to start with, you will not be able to find where you want to go. Prayer seats you in the Presence of God, and then you go from there. Whatever your past experiences are, they cannot be changed. The only thing at our disposal to shape is the present moment. That is the condition of the mind and spirit at the start of prayer and meditation.

I ask God to reveal himself. I know prayer is enjoyable and can become so by simply asking God for revelation and receiving it. We are each a dwelling place of the eternal and Ultimate Truth or Ultimate Divine Consciousness, and fellowshipping with God, in joy, is the essential prayer. A lifestyle of prayer and meditation requires sacrifice, but there is no greater joy nor privilege. Give God all your concerns, fears, wrongdoings and pain. Otherwise, if you don't, then they may impair prayer and impede love. This is an opportunity to seek help if you are caught in a snare that prevents peace. This kind of humility helps prevent the destructive cycle of doing good works with your natural abilities but maintaining harmful life choices and not seeking forgiveness—i.e., living in a self-gratifying, selfish way that can spiral downward into evil. The process of connecting with the Voice is simple. Why miss out on the joy and peace it brings?

I have come to understand and feel that these prayer times are the most cherished by the Voice. In my meditation, I ask for help to be able to think about and seek God continuously. I find it helps to focus and set my mind on God, to see God in my heart, whether or not I am alone. I do this by expressing my adoration, asking for forgiveness of my adverse behaviors and omissions, and praying for the cleansing of my soul.

When I begin prayerful meditation, I start with a breath prayer which eases me into the inner sanctum of the realm that is in all of us.

Not everyone will find the "ambrosial hours" (3:30-5:30 a.m.) to be ideal for their schedule. Instead, do what works for you, setting aside 10-30 minutes for this every day, during a time you will not be interrupted.

The key to successful prayer and meditation is time allotment, no matter which method you choose.

Please find a teacher or a guide to help you in this process. This is such an important and personal matter that I do not presume to provide detailed instruction on this for you. There are entire books and professions devoted to this important matter, so please do consult one of these resources. I can only give you my method, and you can choose to adopt from it what may help you.

Sit quietly and comfortably, though you can also walk instead, if that helps you. Initially, I focus on slowing my breathing and engage in a breath prayer. I do this several times until I begin to feel a stillness, and then I turn my heart inward to this Divine realm. Some will struggle with restlessness in their mind or pain in their body. When I do have discomfort in my body, I briefly place my hand on that body part to acknowledge it, then continue onward without having to think about it any further. If your mind has random thoughts, then just imagine them floating away. This requires practice and time. Coaching from someone you trust to help you with prayer and meditation can be helpful to deal with a restless mind. If you practice for just ten minutes a day for a month, you will notice a difference in your capacity for peace, joy and love. Just continue this practice, increasing the time of your prayers a little each time, and draw from this well. As time goes by, you will realize you cannot live without the deep peace and joy you now know because of this practice. Each person has eternity in their heart; find it by walking this path of prayer.

COMMON PRAYERS

1 - Breath Prayer examples:

Slowly breathe in and out and quietly and silently say your name for God, Source or Eternal Truth in one or two syllables so that you complete the name with an inhale and an exhale. You can also use such two-part phrases as: love – kindness; peace – joy; or You're in me – we are one.

As I am drawn into this peaceful realm, I express my gratitude for the free will I have been given. I ask God to always be inside me and be with me and all around me and never leave me. I tell God how grateful I am when I can feel His tangible presence. I remind myself to ask God to bless my loved ones and to help me know how to help the under-privileged. I express gratitude for those people who have helped me gain a greater understanding of Divine Truth and Ultimate Reality. I ask

God to continually reveal more and more to me of what my purpose in life is, and I ask for help in carrying it out. I ask God to use my life in whatever manner serves love, and to enable me to be obedient to the special personal calling given into my trust. I want to always remember to choose prayer for every question and endeavor I have.

Every day, just before I start my daily works, I seek alignment of my heart, my mind, and my plans for the day; then I say my morning prayer.

2 - My Morning Prayer Example:

Oh God, our Heavenly Father
You are Omnipresent, Omniscient, Alpha, Omega, Immutable and Above All!
Your wondrous acts of love, creation, forgiveness, compassion, redemption, providing, care, grace and everything you do are beyond human capability to comprehend fully to put in adequate words of praise!
Lord, we praise You for everything you do and what You are.
Heavenly Father, please forgive our sins committed, knowingly or unknowingly,
confessed or not confessed, intentional or unintentional.
While seeking forgiveness I am sincerely repenting too.
Father, we thank You for Your forgiveness.
For whatever You have done in my life, whatever You are doing in our lives and whatever You will be doing in our lives, we thank You.

MODEL PRAYERS AND MEDITATIONS FROM VARIOUS RELIGIONS

Throughout history, the Voice has inspired many to pen their longings, adorations, expressions of love, repentance, joy and desire for communion with the Divine. Many of these "spirit words" are touching and are reproduced here for your inspiration, as they have inspired me and helped me to grow in wisdom, love and oneness.

1 - Indigenous People's Prayer for Loss of a Loved One: [101]

At the funeral of _____ (name) say:

Now we become reconciled as you start away. You were once a _____ (occupation) and the People trusted you. Now we release you for it is true that it is no longer possible for us to walk about together on the earth. Now, therefore, we lay the body here. Here we lay it away—we have treated your earthly body with respect.

Now then we say to you, Persevere onward to the place where the Creator dwells in peace. Let not the things of the earth hinder you. Let nothing that transpired while yet you lived hinder you. In _____(activity done with joy) you once took delight; in the game of _____ you once took delight and in the feasts and pleasant occasions your mind was amused, but now do not allow thoughts of these things to give you trouble. Let not your relatives hinder you and also let not your friends and associates trouble your mind. Regard none of these things.

(This writing can be used at funerals as a solemn but joyful way to mark someone's life. It can be printed in a program and read aloud by the audience.)

2 - On the Goal of Meditation – Islamic Sufism

I behold the Light and fix my gaze upon it until I become the Light.

This is a meditation as practiced by Al-Nuri, a ninth century Islamic Sufi Mystic, who learned meditation from a cat he noticed to be intently observing a mouse hole; he learned how to totally quiet his body and focus from her. Al-Nuri emphasized that evil is the absence of light.[102]

3 - Prayer for Wisdom and an Honorable Posterity – Islamic prayer

---

[101] From the Constitution of the Iroquois Nation, Section 1.15.

[102] Sacred Texts -the Mystics of Islam 1914 https://sacred-texts.com/isl/moi/moi.htm

My Lord! Vouchsafe me wisdom and unite me to the righteous.
And give unto me a good report in later generations.
And place me among the inheritors of the Garden of Delight.[103]

4 - On the Importance of Truth in Prayer - Sikhism [104]

Thou shalt not go to Heaven by lip service; it is by the practice of truth thou shalt be delivered.

There are five prayers, five times for prayer, and five names for them—

The first should be truth, the second what is right, the third charity in God's name, the fourth good intentions, the fifth the praise and glory of God.

5 - Model Prayer for Your Unique Destiny and Purpose – Christian

We thank you for your Son, Lord Jesus Christ, and Holy Spirit, and your manifestations through people, places, events and so many ways you have graciously chosen to give us your word, will, wisdom, calling, direction, power, blessing and everything that is needed to understand and obey you and fulfill your unique purpose for our lives.

—Anonymous

(This can be a daily prayer for the Presence of God; the expectations of continual guidance He gives; the mentors and teachers He inhabits, whoever they may be; and for the wisdom for His purposes. Engaging in this prayer can be especially helpful at the beginning of a fresh project for God or when you meet any person, as all people are inhabited by the Spirit of God. And this is an opportunity to reflect the Spirit of God back to someone else in whatever way God wants to.)

---

[103] Quran 26:83-85 (trans. Pickthall).

[104] https://archive.org/details/thesikhreligion01macauoft/page/n133/mode/2up Life of Guru Nanak 1909 Macauliffe

6 - Prayer for Intimacy with God and Intercession for Others – Christian

We thank you for the opportunity you give us to develop personal intimacy with you and with our free will, with the understanding gained for all these, especially from the teachings of Lord Jesus Christ.

I am prayerfully asking you to always please be in me, please be with me, please be all around me and please do not leave me under any circumstances. I need your grace, presence, and everything you can give in every thought, work, and action and every moment of my life.

Also, I pray you bless and transform me, giving total oneness with you. I pray for the ones near and dear to me, and for the ones that showed me the path to you, who have helped me understand the importance of intimacy with you, and will be helping me attain oneness with you.

I pray you help the leaders of all the nations, the poor, weak, lonely, downtrodden and outcasts, and also myself, to act according to your will with total obedience.

Father I also pray you utilize every moment of my life according to your timing and will. Please help me to be always obedient to you and never yield to unrighteous temptations.

—Anonymous

7 - Prayer to Dedicate My Life to Oneness

I pray you utilize my life for the fulfillment of the task of oneness of humanity with you, the one God, and the entire universe worshipping you in oneness; then all the creation of yours will be in peace and joy with love.

Composed by the author

8 - Daily Prayer Seeking the Presence of God

I thank you and seek your blessings,
*   to bless every moment of our life with:*
*   Beholding your beauty*

Hearing your voice
Experiencing your grace and presence,
And Loving you and loving our neighbors the way You want us to love.
And to be your true witnesses and image on this earth,
And fulfill the calling and purpose for which you have created us.
Composed by the author

9 - Disciple's Prayer (a.k.a. the "Lord's Prayer") – Christianity (Bible, Matthew Chapter 6)

This prayer can be used as a blessing of food or as a second prayer after you have prayed for the blessing of the food:

We thank you, pray and seek your blessing, offering the wonderful words of the prayer Lord Jesus Christ taught us, a prayer that will always be powerful, awesome, precious, and adorable:

Our Father in heaven, hallowed be Your name. Your kingdom come. Your will be done on earth as it is in heaven. Give us this day our daily bread. And forgive us our debts, as we forgive our debtors. And do not lead us into temptation but deliver us from the evil one. For Yours is the kingdom and the power and the glory forever. Amen.

—Introduction by the author

10 - Mantra from Rig Veda – Hinduism

Gayatri Mantra

Om Bhur Bhuvah Suvaha
Tat-savitur Varenyam
Bhargo Devasya Dheemahi
Dhiyo Yonah Prachodayat

(The above is the use of English words to approximate the original Sanskrit sounds and vibrations. The following translation will give an understanding of its meaning, and this mantra can be prayed either by speaking the original Sanskrit or its translation):

I meditate on the Supreme Divine Reality and Source of life who lights all realms and is the highest Truth. I seek divine enlightenment enabling me to follow truth and righteousness. Translation from the Sanskrit is by the author.

11 - Mantra from Tibetan Buddhism

Om Mani Padme Hum!

Translated as: *Oh, Jewel in the lotus flower! Amen!*

(Its utterance is to convey the person praying this directly into the spiritual realm. The English elaboration of the meaning is "Praise to the Jewel that is Wisdom, Love, Purity and Oneness. Amen." Translation of the English elaboration from the Sanskrit is by the author)

12 - Buddhist Prayer and Psalm

Lauding the Infinite One

1. Since He who is Infinite attained unto the Wisdom Supreme, the long, long ages of ten Kalpas have rolled away.

The Light of His Dharma-Kaya is in this world eyes to the blind.

2. Seek refuge in the True Illumination! For the light of His Wisdom is infinite.

In all the worlds there is nothing upon which His light shines not.

3. Take refuge in the Light universal.

As the Light of His deliverance is boundless, he who is within it is freed from the lie of affirmation or denial.

4. Seek refuge in That which is beyond understanding,

For His glory is all-embracing as the air. It shineth and pierceth all things, and there is nothing hid from the light thereof.

5. Take refuge in the ultimate Strength, for His pure radiance is above all things. He who perceiveth this Light is set free from the fetters of Karma.

6. Seek refuge in the World-Honoured.

Since His glorious radiance is above all He is called the Buddha of Divine Light. And by Him is the darkness of the three worlds Enlightened.

7. Excellent is the Light of His Wisdom. Therefore is he called the Buddha of Clear Shining.

He who is within the Light, being washed from the soil of Karma, shall attain unto the final deliverance.

8. Take refuge in the Mighty Consoler. Wheresoever His mercy shineth throughout all the worlds, men rejoice in its gladdening light.

9. The darkness of ignorance perisheth before His light. Therefore is He hailed as the Buddha of Radiant Wisdom. All the Buddhas and the threefold choir of sages praise Him.

10. His glory shineth for ever and ever. Therefore is He called the Buddha of Everlasting Light.

Most excellent is the virtue of this light, for he who perceiveth it is born into Paradise without dissolution of being.[105]

13 - Prayer for Forgiveness and Redemption

Lord, knowingly or unknowingly, intentionally or unintentionally, yielding to temptations of circumstances and situations, people resort to actions that cause physical, emotional, or financial harm to one another. Forgive me for whatever I have done and restore and abundantly reward the ones I have hurt. And I pray you forgive the ones that hurt me.
     —The Author

---

[105] Yamabe, S. and L. Adams Beck, *Wisdom of the East—Buddhist Psalms translated from the Japanese of Shinra Shonin* (https://www.gutenberg.org/cache/epub/7015/pg7015-images.html).

14 – An Atheist's Prayer[106]

(a.k.a. the Wisdom Prayer)

Wisdom stands before me.

I can walk with wisdom for my journey.

I will let wisdom be my teacher and virtue will be my guide as I walk down the path of love.

I will seek to learn from the wisdom of others, and I will let my life be a teacher of wisdom and respect.

I will always seek to respect others and learn from them while being an example of the wisdom I have learned during this life, paid for with time.

I will treat others as I like to be treated, and I will train my children in this way. I will care for my family, and I will be grateful for their love and care for me.

I will not harm anyone physically, emotionally, or financially.

I will help the needy when I can, and I am grateful for the resources that I have to do so.

I will take care of the earth, my home, and respect its gifts and humbly gaze at its beauty.

I am quantum entangled with all in the universe, and I choose to live with respect for nature which has been my home in this life. I will meditate on these good things.

I am grateful for the time I had to learn and live, and I freely give to others my knowledge and my love.

(The above is suitable for reading at any type of significant event such as a wedding, funeral, or any type of solemn occasion, especially when sacred language is desired without assigning religion. The poem can be read by one person or in an alternating responsive way by the audience.)

---

[106] Composed by the author.

15 - Moses' Blessing Prayer – Jewish Scriptures

The LORD bless you, and keep you.
> *The LORD make his face to shine on you,*
> *and be gracious to you.*
> *The LORD lift up his face toward you,*
> *and give you peace.*[107]

16 - Oneness Prayer and Meditations[108]

(May be addressed to True One God, Divine Consciousness, Source, Ultimate Truth or your name for the One God or One Ultimate Reality):

Gratitude
I am grateful for the experience of growing in love as I humbly gaze at the expansive universe in which I dwell and which dwells in me. I will never fully comprehend this amazing world that I look to for wisdom, love and truth.

Self-examination
I will examine myself for harmful tendencies or actions and seek forgiveness and mercy from all I have harmed and in return I extend the same forgiveness and mercy, as I want to live a life without harming others physically, emotionally, or financially, seeking to live in oneness and peace with all others.

Exhortation
I am grateful for the provisions needed for life, the unmerited favor I enjoy, and the noble role models set before me as I work towards being an example of honor, respect and kindness to those near and dear to me as well as the world around me.

---

[107] Numbers 6:24-26 (https://ebible.org/engwmb/NUM06.htm).

[108] Composed by the author.

Humility and Acknowledgment
I will keep an open mind and open heart towards love and truth in all
realms and I will live a life in which truth and love prevail, walking in
humility in this universe, with which I am one.

Thank you, thank you, thank you!

(The above may be read or prayed in its entirety as a single prayer
or each meditation can be individually and deeply contemplated during
a meditation session.)

PASSAGES FROM SCRIPTURES, POETRY AND SONGS OF VARIOUS RELIGIONS, TRADITIONS, FAITHS AND PHILOSOPHIES

As you read through these passages, please pause for a moment of
respect for the inspiration from the eternal realm and for the sacrifices
of those who have gone before us to blaze these trails for the benefit of
us all who seek to walk the spiritual path. What you hold in your hands
is precious—in part because some of these speakers and writers endured
torture, loss of loved ones, emotional agony, imprisonment or even
death just for having written these words.

1 - Excerpts from the *Japji – III* Sikh Scriptures

Great is His Will!!
All manifest things are forms of His Will.
His Will is indefinable!
Of His Will is made all sentient life;
It is His will that some are great, some are small.
All existence is bound by His Supreme Will.
Nothing is outside the sphere of His Will; such is truth!
Seek His Will—this is to live.
If one sees the Universal Will at work, then one can never say "Tis I."

The bards have chanted hymns in praise of Him, His Power, and His Great Gifts, and sung His Signs.[109]

2 - The Hope of a Man of Worth – from the Jewish Tanakh

Proverbs 31 – the advice of a mother to her son to seek a woman of valor!

... the burden wherewith his mother corrected him. What, my son? and what, O son of my womb? and what, O son of my vows?... A woman of valor, who can find? for her price is far above rubies. The heart of her husband does safely trust in her, and he has no lack of gain. She does him good and not evil all the days of her life. She seeks wool and flax, and works willingly with her hands. She is like the merchant-ships; she brings her food from afar. She rises also while it is yet night, and gives food to her household, and a portion to her maidens. She considers a field, and buys it; with the fruit of her hands she plants a vineyard. She girds her loins with strength, and makes strong her arms. She perceives that her merchandise is good; her lamp goes not out by night. She lays her hands to the distaff, and her hands hold the spindle. She stretches out her hand to the poor; yes, she reaches forth her hands to the needy. She is not afraid of the snow for her household; for all her household are clothed with scarlet. She makes for herself coverlets; her clothing is fine linen and purple. Her husband is known in the gates, when he sits among the elders of the land. She makes linen garments and sells them; and delivers girdles unto the merchant. Strength and dignity are her clothing; and she laughs at the time to come. She opens her mouth with wisdom; and the law of kindness is on her tongue. She looks well to the ways of her household, and eats not the bread of idleness. Her children rise up, and call her blessed; her husband also, and he praises her: 'Many daughters have done valiantly, but you excel them all.' Grace is deceitful, and beauty is vain; but a woman

---

[109] Guru Nanak
(https://archive.org/details/gurunanaksjapjiandsohilaartiprof.puransingh/page/n5/mode/2up).

that fears the LORD, she shall be praised. Give her of the fruit of her hands; and let her works praise her in the gates.

Excerpts from Proverbs 31 with modernized english.[110]

3 - Knowing Your Prayer Will Be Heard – from Jewish scriptures

The sacrifices of God are a broken spirit.
O God, you will not despise a broken and contrite heart.[111]

4 - Tenrikyo Literature

Song V

First,
As this world is so wide,
There may be various places to save people.
Second,
Miraculous salvation at this place,
I grant you safe childbirth and freedom from smallpox.
Third,
God, the same as water,
Washes away the dirt from your minds.
Fourth,
Though there is no one who is free from greed, Before God there is no greed.
Fifth,
However long you may continue to believe,
Your life shall ever be filled with joy.
Sixth,
Forgetting away a cruel heart,
Come to Me with a gentle heart!

---

[110] https://ebible.org/engjps/PRO31.htm

[111] Psalm 51:17 (https://ebible.org/engwmb/PSA051.htm).

Seventh,
Assuredly I shall never leave you in suffering,
Because this is the place of single-hearted salvation.
Eighth,
Not only in Yamato,
I will go also to other countries to save you all.
Ninth,
This is the Jiba, the origin of this world.
Indeed a remarkable place has been revealed.

Since firmly we are determined to believe,
Let us form a brotherhood.[112]

5 - Quotes from the *Analects of Confucius*[113]

Book 1

"Let young people," said he, "show filial piety at home, respectfulness towards their elders when away from home; let them be circumspect, be truthful; their love going out freely towards all, cultivating good-will to men. And if, in such a walk, there be time or energy left for other things, let them employ it in the acquisition of literary or artistic accomplishments."

A saying of the Scholar Tsang:—"The virtue of the people is renewed and enriched when attention is seen to be paid to the departed, and the remembrance of distant ancestors kept and cherished."

Tsz-kung asked, "What say you, sir, of the poor who do not cringe and fawn; and what of the rich who are without pride and haughtiness?" "They are passable," the Master replied; "yet they are scarcely in the same category as the poor who are happy, and the rich who love propriety."

---

[112] https://archive.org/details/mikagura-uta-the-songs-for-the-service./page/12/mode/2up.

[113] Excerpts from *Analects* Books 1-5 Translators: Sir John Francis Davis, William Jennings and James Legge

https://www.gutenberg.org/cache/epub/10056/pg10056-images.html

Book 2

Let a ruler base his government upon virtuous principles, and he will be like the pole-star, which remains steadfast in its place, while all the host of stars turn towards it.

"The 'Book of Odes' contains three hundred pieces, but one expression in it may be taken as covering the purport of all, viz., Unswerving mindfulness."

To the disciple Tsz-lu the Master said, "Shall I give you a lesson about knowledge? When you know a thing, maintain that you know it; and when you do not, acknowledge your ignorance. This is characteristic of knowledge."

Book 3

Of "the superior man," the Master observed, "In him there is no contentiousness. Say even that he does certainly contend with others, as in archery competitions; yet mark, in that case, how courteously he will bow and go up for the forfeit-cup, and come down again and give it to his competitor. In his very contest he is still the superior man."

Wang-sun Kis asked him once, "What says the proverb, 'Better to court favor in the kitchen than in the drawing-room'?" The Master replied, "Nay, better say, He who has sinned against Heaven has none other to whom prayer may be addressed."

Book 4

Riches and honor are what men desire; but if they arrive at them by improper ways, they should not continue to hold them. Poverty and low estate are what men dislike; but if they arrive at such a condition by improper ways, they should not refuse it.

The scholar who is intent upon learning the right way, and who is yet ashamed of poor attire and poor food, is not worthy of being discoursed with.

Where there is habitual going after gain, there is much ill-will.

One should not be greatly concerned at not being in office; but rather about the requirements in one's self for such a standing. Neither should one be so much concerned at being unknown; but rather with seeking to become worthy of being known.

To be slow to speak, but prompt to act, is the desire of the 'superior man.'

Book 5

"My attitude towards a man in my first dealings with him," he added, "was to listen to his professions and to trust to his conduct. My attitude now is to listen to his professions, and to watch his conduct."

That which I do not wish others to put upon me, I also wish not to put upon others.

6 - The Great Supreme – Taoist Literature

CHAPTER VI[114]

Argument—

He who knows what God is, and who knows what Man is, has attained. Knowing what God is, he knows that he himself proceeded therefrom. Knowing what Man is, he rests in the knowledge of the known, waiting for the knowledge of the unknown. Working out one's allotted span, and not perishing in mid career—this is the fulness of knowledge.

God is a principle which exists by virtue of its own intrinsicality, and operates spontaneously, without self-manifestation.

It is in the human that the divine finds expression. Man emanates from God, and should therefore be on earth, in this brief life of ours, what God is for all eternity in the universe.

Herein, however, there is a flaw. Knowledge is dependent upon

---

[114] Chuang Tzu, *Chuang Tzu: Mystic, Moralist, and Social Reformer,* translated from the Chinese by Herbert A. Giles (https://www.gutenberg.org/cache/epub/59709/pg59709-images.html#Page_68).

fulfilment. And as this fulfilment is uncertain, how can it be known that my divine is not really human, my human really divine?

Not until death lifts the veil can we truly know that this life is bounded at each end by an immortality to which the soul finally reverts.

"Heaven from all creatures hides the book of Fate,
All but the page prescribed, their present state."

7 - Stoicism – *The Meditations of the Emperor Marcus Aurelius Antoninus*[115]

Book II.

1. Say this to yourself in the morning: Today I shall have to do with meddlers, with the ungrateful, with the insolent, with the crafty, with the envious and the selfish. All these vices have beset them, because they know not what is good and what is evil. But I have considered the nature of the good, and found it beautiful: I have beheld the nature of the bad, and found it ugly. I also understand the nature of the evil-doer, and know that he is my brother, not because he shares with me the same blood or the same seed, but because he is a partaker of the same mind and of the same portion of immortality. I therefore cannot be hurt by any of these, since none of them can involve me in any baseness. I cannot be angry with my brother, or sever myself from him, for we are made by nature for mutual assistance, like the feet, the hands, the eyelids, the upper and lower rows of teeth. It is against nature for men to oppose each other; and what else is anger and aversion?

8 - On the Benefits of Oneness of Humanity from the Islamic Scriptures – the Quran[116]

The Believers, men and women, are protectors one of another: they enjoin

---

[115] Chriystal, George W., The Meditations of the Emperor Marcus Aurelius Antoninus: A new rendering based on the Foulis translation of 1742 (https://www.gutenberg.org/files/55317/55317-h/55317-h.htm).

[116] Quran 9:71 (trans. Abdullah Yusuf Ali). (https://www.gutenberg.org/cache/epub/16955/pg16955-images.html).

what is just, and forbid what is evil: they observe regular prayers, practise regular charity, and obey Allah and His Messenger. On them will Allah pour His mercy: for Allah is Exalted in Power, Wise.

9 - Buddhist Psalm of Paradise[117]

Seek refuge in the heavenly harmony.

For the jewel groves and gem trees of Paradise give forth a sweet and most excellent melody in pure and ordered unison.

Seek refuge in the Divine Promise, the Treasury of Merit,

For the seven jewel trees are fragrant in Paradise where the flowers, the fruits, the branches and the leaves thereof

Cast back their radiance the one to the other.

Bring homage to the perfect Righteousness.

As the pure wind blows over the trees glorious with jewels,

It draweth from them a noble music with five-fold strains of harmony.

In all the world is no place hidden from the glory shed by hundreds of myriad rays from the heart of every flower of Paradise.

Like unto a golden mountain reflecting the myriad rays of these heavenly blossoms, so is the form of the Infinite One.

From His Sacred Body, as from a well-spring, floweth this light over the Ten Regions of the world.

By His Sacred teaching He leadeth all having life into the way of light.

Seek refuge in the Treasury of Righteousness.

For in Paradise is that holy lake, with its waters of eightfold Virtue, all-glorious with the seven jewels. And all this is the inconceivable handiwork of Purity.

Seek refuge in the All-Honoured.

For when sorrow and sighing are fled away, the Holy Land shall rejoice with joy and singing. Therefore is it called Paradise.

The Buddhas of the Three Ages and the Ten Regions, they in whom the

---

[117] From Buddhist Psalms translated from the Japanese of Shinran Shonin by S. Yamabe and L. Adams Beck (https://www.gutenberg.org/cache/epub/7015/pg7015-images.html).

Dual Wisdom is perfect and their illumination entire, lead all the worlds marvellously into the way of Salvation, the Truth being their Vehicle.

He that seeketh refuge in the Kingdom of the Infinite One is a citizen of the Kingdom of every Buddha.

Let him that is set free, with single heart give praises unto One Buddha, for in so doing he praiseth all.

The faithful believer at that moment when he rejoiceth in the sound of the name of the Infinite One hath revealed unto his very eyes the Buddha of Light.

Let him that hath faith praise the Virtue of the Divine Wisdom.

Let him strive to declare it unto all men that he may offer his thankfulness for the grace of the Buddha.

10 - On Not Worrying and Laying Up Treasures in Heaven – Christian Scriptures

Luke 12:22-40[118]

He (Jesus) said to his disciples, "Therefore I tell you, don't be anxious for your life, what you will eat, nor yet for your body, what you will wear. Life is more than food, and the body is more than clothing. Consider the ravens: they don't sow, they don't reap, they have no warehouse or barn, and God feeds them. How much more valuable are you than birds! Which of you by being anxious can add a cubit to his height? If then you aren't able to do even the least things, why are you anxious about the rest? Consider the lilies, how they grow. They don't toil, neither do they spin; yet I tell you, even Solomon in all his glory was not arrayed like one of these. But if this is how God clothes the grass in the field, which today exists and tomorrow is cast into the oven, how much more will he clothe you, O you of little faith?

"Don't seek what you will eat or what you will drink; neither be anxious. For the nations of the world seek after all of these things, but your Father knows that you need these things. But seek God's Kingdom, and all these things will be added to you.

---

[118] https://ebible.org/engwmb/LUK12.htm.

"Don't be afraid, little flock, for it is your Father's good pleasure to give you the Kingdom. Sell what you have and give gifts to the needy. Make for yourselves purses which don't grow old, a treasure in the heavens that doesn't fail, where no thief approaches and no moth destroys. For where your treasure is, there will your heart be also.

11 - Heaven and Earth Endure, *Tao Te Ching* – Taoism

Chapter 7[119]

> *Heaven is long-enduring and earth continues long.*
> *The reason why Heaven and earth are able to endure and continue thus long*
> *is because they do not live of, or for, themselves.*
> *This is how they are able to continue and endure.*
> *Therefore, the sage puts his own person last,*
> *and yet it is found in the foremost place;*
> *he treats his person as if it were foreign to him,*
> *and yet that person is preserved.*
> *Is it not because he has no personal and private ends,*
> *that therefore such ends are realised?*

12 - The Seed Bestowed on Them by the Gods of Heaven - Shintoism (Description from Oral Renderings)

Anciently the Mikado received the auspicious grain from the Gods of Heaven, and therewithal nourished the people. In the Daijôwe (or Ohonihe) the Mikado, when the grain became ripe, joined unto him the people in sincere veneration, and, as in duty bound, made return to the Gods of Heaven. He thereafter partook of it along with the nation. Thus the people learnt that the grain which they eat is no other than the seed bestowed on them by the Gods of Heaven.[120]

---

[119] https://www.gutenberg.org/cache/epub/216/pg216-images.html trans Legge

[120] Aston, W.G., Shinto: *The Ancient Religion of Japan*, (London: Constable & Company Ltd., 1921).

13 - *Bhagavad Gita* (the Song of God) – Hindu Scriptures

Chapter XII[121]

Arjuna:
Lord! Of the men who serve Thee—true in heart—
As God revealed; and of the men who serve,
Worshipping Thee Unrevealed, Unbodied, Far,
Which take the better way of faith and life?
Krishna:
Whoever serve Me—as I show Myself—
Constantly true, in full devotion fixed,
Those hold I very holy. But who serve—
Worshipping Me The One, The Invisible,
The Unrevealed, Unnamed, Unthinkable,
Uttermost, All-pervading, Highest, Sure—
Who thus adore Me, mastering their sense,
Of one set mind to all, glad in all good,
These blessed souls come unto Me.
Yet, hard
The travail is for such as bend their minds
To reach th' Unmanifest That viewless path
Shall scarce be trod by man bearing the flesh!
But whereso any doeth all his deeds
Renouncing self for Me, full of Me, fixed
To serve only the Highest, night and day
Musing on Me—him will I swiftly lift
Forth from life's ocean of distress and death,
Whose soul clings fast to Me. Cling thou to Me!
Clasp Me with heart and mind! So shalt thou dwell
Surely with Me on high. But if thy thought
Droops from such height; if thou be'st weak to set
Body and soul upon Me constantly,

---

[121] https://www.gutenberg.org/files/2388/2388-h/2388-h.htm#chap12.

Despair not! Give Me lower service! Seek
To reach Me, worshipping with steadfast will;
And, if thou canst not worship steadfastly,
Work for Me, toil in works pleasing to Me!
For he that laboureth right for love of Me
Shall finally attain! But, if in this
Thy faint heart fails, bring Me thy failure! Find
Refuge in Me! let fruits of labour go,
Renouncing hope for Me, with lowliest heart,
So shalt thou come; for, though to know is more
Than diligence, yet worship better is
Than knowing, and renouncing better still.
Near to renunciation—very near—
Dwelleth Eternal Peace!

That man I love! Who troubleth not his kind,
And is not troubled by them; clear of wrath,
Living too high for gladness, grief, or fear,
That man I love! Who, dwelling quiet-eyed,
Stainless, serene, well-balanced, unperplexed,
Working with Me, yet from all works detached,
That man I love! Who, fixed in faith on Me,
Dotes upon none, scorns none; rejoices not,
And grieves not, letting good or evil hap
Light when it will, and when it will depart,
That man I love! Who, unto friend and foe
Keeping an equal heart, with equal mind
Bears shame and glory; with an equal peace
Takes heat and cold, pleasure and pain; abides
Quit of desires, hears praise or calumny
In passionless restraint, unmoved by each;
Linked by no ties to earth, steadfast in Me,
That man I love! But most of all I love
Those happy ones to whom 'tis life to live

In single fervid faith and love unseeing,
Drinking the blessed Amrit of my Being!

14 - The Magnificat (Mary's Song)[122] – Christian Scriptures

My soul magnifies the Lord.
My spirit has rejoiced in God my Savior,
for he has looked at the humble state of his servant.
For behold, from now on, all generations will call me blessed.
For he who is mighty has done great things for me.
Holy is his name.
His mercy is for generations and generations on those who fear him.
He has shown strength with his arm.
He has scattered the proud in the imagination of their hearts.
He has put down princes from their thrones,
and has exalted the lowly.
He has filled the hungry with good things.
He has sent the rich away empty.
He has given help to Israel, his servant, that he might remember mercy,
as he spoke to our fathers,
to Abraham and his offspring forever.

15 - He is One. He is the First, *Guru Nanak's Japji*[123] – Sikhism

He is One. He is the First. He is all that is.
His name is Truth.
He is the Creator of all.
Fearing naught, striking fear in naught; His Form, on lands and waters, is Eternity; the One Self-existent.
Through the Grace of His true servant, continually repeat His Name.

---

[122] Luke 1:46-55, Mary's words upon learning she is carrying the child of God. (https://ebible.org/engwmb/LUK01.htm).

[123] Guru Nanak, trans. Puran Singh, *Guru Nanak's Japji and Sohila Arti* (https://archive.org/details/gurunanaksjapjiandsohilaartiprof.puransingh/page/n3/mode/2up).

He was in the beginning; He is through all ages, He shall be the One who lives for ever.

Beyond thought, no thinking can conceive Him, not even if the minds of men should think for ages and ages.

Nor silence can see him, even if the minds of men meditate on Him for ages and ages.

Nor can He be known by gaining the worlds: for man's desire is never satiated, even though all the worlds laden with gold fall to his share.

Nor human thoughts can carry man far.

The movements of his mind, the thousand acts of wisdom of the world, leave him dark; nothing avails.

Vain are the ways of men.

How then to find Him?

How then to get rid of the dark pall?

One way there is, to make His Will our own. No other way, naught else.

16 - The Love Chapter[124] – Christian Scriptures

If I speak with the languages of men and of angels, but don't have love, I have become sounding brass or a clanging cymbal. If I have the gift of prophecy, and know all mysteries and all knowledge, and if I have all faith, so as to remove mountains, but don't have love, I am nothing. If I give away all my goods to feed the poor, and if I give my body to be burned, but don't have love, it profits me nothing.

Love is patient and is kind. Love doesn't envy. Love doesn't brag, is not proud, doesn't behave itself inappropriately, doesn't seek its own way, is not provoked, takes no account of evil; doesn't rejoice in unrighteousness, but rejoices with the truth; bears all things, believes all things, hopes all things, and endures all things.

Love never fails. But where there are prophecies, they will be done away with. Where there are various languages, they will cease. Where there is knowledge, it will be done away with. For we know in part and we prophesy in part; but when that which is complete has come, then that which is

---

[124] 1 Corinthians 13:1-13 (WMB World Messianic Bible).

partial will be done away with. When I was a child, I spoke as a child, I felt as a child, I thought as a child. Now that I have become a man, I have put away childish things. For now we see in a mirror, dimly, but then face to face. Now I know in part, but then I will know fully, even as I was also fully known. But now faith, hope, and love remain—these three. The greatest of these is love.

17 - I Will See God, *Book of Job*[125] – Jewish Scriptures

23 Oh that my words were now written! Oh that they were inscribed in a book! 24 That with an iron pen and lead they were graven in the rock for ever! 25 But as for me, I know that my Redeemer liveth, and that He will witness at the last upon the dust; 26 And when after my skin this is destroyed, then without my flesh shall I see God; 27 Whom I, even I, shall see for myself, and mine eyes shall behold, and not another's.

18 - Praise for "No matter what happens!" – Jewish Scriptures

Habakkuk[126]
17 For though the fig-tree shall not blossom, neither shall fruit be in the vines; the labour of the olive shall fail, and the fields shall yield no food; the flock shall be cut off from the fold, and there shall be no herd in the stalls; 18 Yet I will rejoice in the LORD, I will exult in the God of my salvation. 19 God, the Lord, is my strength, and He maketh my feet like hinds' feet, and He maketh me to walk upon my high places.

19 – Al Infatar (the Cleaving Asunder) [127] – Islamic Scriptures

When the Sky is cleft asunder;
When the Stars are scattered;
When the Oceans are suffered to burst forth;

---

[125] Job 19:23-27 (JPS Tanakh 1917).

[126] Habbukuk 3:17-19 (JPS Tanakh 1917).

[127] Quran 82:1-19, Surah Al-Infatar (trans. Yusuf).

And when the Graves are turned upside down;

[Then] shall each soul know what it hath sent forward and [what it hath] kept back.

O man! What has seduced thee from thy Lord Most Beneficent?

Him Who created thee. Fashioned thee in due proportion, and gave thee a just bias;

In whatever Form He wills, does He put thee together.

20 - Desire Wisdom, from *The Book of Wisdom*[128] – Jewish Septuagint (Greek translation of original Hebrew Scriptures) and Christian Scriptures, Excerpts from Chapter 6

13. Wisdom is glorious, and never fadeth away, and is easily seen by them that love her, and is found by them that seek her.

14. She preventeth them that covet her, so that she first sheweth herself unto them.

15. He that awaketh early to seek her, shall not labour: for he shall find her sitting at his door.

16. To think, therefore, upon her, is perfect understanding: and he that watcheth for her, shall quickly be secure.

17. For she goeth about seeking such as are worthy of her, and she sheweth herself to them cheerfully in the ways, and meeteth them with all providence.

18. For the beginning of her is the most true desire of discipline.

19. And the care of discipline is love: and love is the keeping of her laws: and the keeping of her laws is the firm foundation of incorruption:

20. And incorruption bringeth near to God.

21. Therefore the desire of wisdom bringeth to the everlasting kingdom.

22. If then your delight be in thrones, and sceptres, O ye kings of the people, love wisdom, that you may reign for ever.

23. Love the light of wisdom, all ye that bear rule over peoples.

24. Now what wisdom is, and what was her origin, I will declare: and I will not hide from you the mysteries of God, but will seek her out from the

---

[128] Wisdom of Solomon 6:13-23 (Douay-Rheims Version).

beginning of her birth, and bring the knowledge of her to light, and will not pass over the truth:

21 - Al-Baqara[129] – Islamic Scriptures Quran

O ye people! Adore your Guardian-Lord, who created you and those who came before you, that ye may have the chance to learn righteousness;

Who has made the earth your couch, and the heavens your canopy; and sent down rain from the heavens; and brought forth therewith Fruits for your sustenance; then set not up rivals unto Allah when ye know (the truth).

And if ye are in doubt as to what We have revealed from time to time to Our servant, then produce a Sura like thereunto; and call your witnesses or helpers (If there are any) besides Allah, if your (doubts) are true.

But if ye cannot—and of a surety ye cannot—then fear the Fire whose fuel is men and stones, which is prepared for those who reject Faith.

But give glad tidings to those who believe and work righteousness, that their portion is Gardens, beneath which rivers flow. Every time they are fed with fruits therefrom, they say: "Why, this is what we were fed with before," for they are given things in similitude; and they have therein companions pure (and holy); and they abide therein (for ever).

22 - All in One, *Isa Upanishad*[130] – Hindu Scriptures

He who sees all beings in the Self and the Self in all beings, he never turns away from It (the Self).

He who perceives all beings as the Self for him how can there be delusion or grief, when he sees this oneness (everywhere)?

He who perceives the Self everywhere never shrinks from anything, because through his higher consciousness he feels united with all life. When a man sees God in all beings and all beings in God, and also God dwelling

---

[129] Quran 2:21-25 (trans. Yusuf).

[130] Isa Upanishad 6-8, translated with commentary by Swami Paramandanda (https://www.gutenberg.org/cache/epub/3283/pg3283.html).

in his own Soul, how can he hate any living thing? Grief and delusion rest upon a belief in diversity, which leads to competition and all forms of selfishness. With the realization of oneness, the sense of diversity vanishes and the cause of misery is removed.

He (the Self) is all-encircling, resplendent, bodiless, spotless, without sinews, pure, untouched by sin, all-seeing, all-knowing, transcendent, self-existent; He has disposed all things duly for eternal years.

23 - Praise, Worship, Wisdom and Righteousness[131] – Zoroastrian Scriptures

Excerpts from *Yasna 31*, Declaration of Praise for the Unchanging One God

6. The very best (reward) shall be his who knowing it, can tell me aright the word of Righteousness in reference to the Eternal Welfare and Immortality; yea (as reward) the Kingdom of Mazda (Supreme God) which by his Good Mind he increases for Him.

7. (Mazda) who in the beginning conceived the thought to fill His heavenly realms with light— He by His wisdom founder of Righteousness (the Law), by which to keep up His Best Mind (in His people); these blessed realms mayest Thou with Thy Spirit increase,

Thou, O Ahura Mazda, who art even until now (and forever) unchanging.

8. 'Therefore in the beginning, O Mazda,

I conceived Thee in mind to be worthy of worship, when I beheld Thee in mine eye,

as the father of the Good Mind,

the very founder of Asha, the Law of Righteousness, the Lord amid the deeds of life.

11. 'Since Thou, O Mazda (Supreme God), in the beginning for us

---

[131] Zend-Avesta, Public domain "A Hymn of Zoroaster- Yasna 31", by Willams Jackson, Abraham Valentine 1862-1937

our beings and consciences hast formed and our intelligence through Thine Own mind, since Thou madest life clothed with a body, since Thou gavest us the works and words whereby one freely may express his belief,

12. So lifts up his voice (alike) the false prophet and the true, the foolish and the wise, according to his heart and mind;

17. 'Which of the two—that which the righteous or the wicked believes—is the greater? Let the enlightened to the enlightened speak, nor let the unenlightened deceive; be Thou to us, O Ahura Mazda, the revealer of Thy Good Mind

24 - Praise[132] – Islamic Scriptures, Quran 67:1-3

Blessed be He in Whose hands is Dominion; and He over all things hath Power;

He Who created Death and Life, that He may try which of you is best in deed: and He is the Exalted in Might, Oft-Forgiving;

He Who created the seven heavens one above another: No want of proportion wilt thou see in the Creation of (Allah) Most Gracious. So turn thy vision again: seest thou any flaw?

25 - A Psalm of Comfort[133] – Jewish Scriptures

Psalm 23, A Psalm of David.

The LORD is my shepherd; I shall not want. 2 He maketh me to lie down in green pastures; He leadeth me beside the still waters. 3 He restoreth my soul; He guideth me in straight paths for His name's sake. 4 Yea, though I walk through the valley of the shadow of death, I will fear no evil, for Thou art with me; Thy rod and Thy staff, they comfort me. 5 Thou preparest a table before me in the presence of mine enemies; Thou hast anointed my head with oil; my cup runneth over. 6 Surely goodness and

---

[132] Qur'an 67:1-3 (trans. Yusuf).

[133] Psalm 23:1-6 (JPS Tanakh 1917).

mercy shall follow me all the days of my life; and I shall dwell in the house of the LORD forever.

26 - *Tattvartha Sutra* – Jainism

I bow to the Lord, the promulgator of the path to liberation, the destroyer of mountains of karmas and the knower of the whole of reality, so that I may realize these qualities.

Right faith, right knowledge, and right conduct (together) constitute the path to liberation.[134]

27 - The Beatitudes[135] – Christian Scriptures

Seeing the multitudes, he went up onto the mountain.
When he had sat down, his disciples came to him.
He opened his mouth and taught them, saying,
"Blessed are the poor in spirit,
for theirs is the Kingdom of Heaven.
Blessed are those who mourn,
for they shall be comforted.
Blessed are the gentle,
for they shall inherit the earth.
Blessed are those who hunger and thirst for righteousness,
for they shall be filled.
Blessed are the merciful,
for they shall obtain mercy.
Blessed are the pure in heart,
for they shall see God.
Blessed are the peacemakers,
for they shall be called children of God.
1Blessed are those who have been persecuted for righteousness' sake,

---

[134] Tattvartha Sutra (trans. Trans. Acharya Umaswati Public Domain
https://archive.org/details/tattvarthbook10webf/page/n27/mode/2up
[135] Matthew 5:3-10 (World Messianic Bible).

for theirs is the Kingdom of Heaven.

28 - The Journey of a Thousand Miles, *Tao Te Ching*[136] – Taoism

62
The Tao is the tabernacle of creation,
it is a treasure for those who are good,
and a place of refuge for those who are not.
When a new leader takes office, don't give him gifts and offerings. These things are not as valuable as teaching him about the Tao.
Why was the Tao esteemed by the ancient Masters?
Is it not said: "With it we find without looking. With it we find forgiveness for our transgressions."
That is why the world cannot understand it.
64
Things are easier to control while things are quiet.
Prevent problems before they arise.
Take action before things get out of hand. The tallest tree
begins as a tiny sprout.
The tallest building
starts with one shovel of dirt.
A journey of a thousand miles
starts with a single footstep.
If you rush into action, you will fail.
If you hold on too tight, you will lose your grip.
By pursuing your goals too relentlessly,
you let them slip away.
If you are as concerned about the outcome
as you are about the beginning,
then it is hard to do things wrong.
The master seeks no possessions.
She learns by unlearning,

---

[136] *Tao Te Ching* excerpts (trans. JH McDonald 1996 Public Domain)

thus she is able to understand all things.
This gives her the ability to help all of creation.

29 - Vedic Hymns to the Unknown God[137] – Hindu Scriptures

In the beginning there arose the Golden Child. As soon as born, he alone was the lord of all that is. He established the earth and this heaven—Who is the God to whom we shall offer sacrifice?

He who gives breath, he who gives strength, whose command all the bright gods revere, whose shadow is immortality, whose shadow is death— Who is the God to whom we shall offer sacrifice?

He who through his might became the sole king of the breathing and twinkling world, who governs all this, man and beast:—Who is the God to whom we shall offer sacrifice?

He through whose might these snowy mountains are, and the sea, they say, with the distant river; he of whom these regions are indeed the two arms—Who is the God to whom we shall offer sacrifice?

He through whom the awful heaven and the earth were made fast, he through whom the ether was established, and the firmament; he who measured the air in the sky—Who is the God to whom we shall offer sacrifice?

He to whom heaven and earth, standing firm by his will, look up, trembling in their mind; he over whom the risen sun shines forth:—Who is the God to whom we shall offer sacrifice?

When the great waters went everywhere, holding the germ, and generating light, then there arose from them the breath of the god:—Who is the God to whom we shall offer sacrifice?

He who by his might looked even over the waters which held power and generated the sacrifice, he who alone is God above all gods—Who is the God to whom we shall offer sacrifice?

May he not hurt us, he who is the begetter of the earth, or he, the righteous, who begat the heaven; he who also begat the bright and mighty waters—Who is the God to whom we shall offer sacrifice?

---

[137] Rig Veda 10:121:1-10 (trans. Müller).

Pragâpati, no other than thou embraces all these created things. May that be ours which we desire when sacrificing to thee: may we be lords of wealth!

30 - Praise to the Supreme God, The Waaqeffanna Song – African Indigenous Spirituality (Waaqeffanna Religion)

"O wonder! O wonder! . . . The wonders are six: The hornbill complains without being sick; the plant flourishes without nourishment; the water runs without being urged; the earth is fixed without pegs; the heavens hold themselves up without supports; in the firmament He (God) has sown the chick-peas of heaven. These things fill me with wonder. Let us all pray to God! O God, who hast caused me to pass the day cause me to pass the night well!"[138]

31 - Invocation for Good Fortune – African Indigenous Ifa Religion

ORIKI EJIOGBE

(Invocation for Good Fortune)

Ejiogbe, Ejiogbe, Ejiogbe. Mo be yin, kiegbe mi ki'mi niyi, ki e egbe mi ki'mi n'ola, ifakifa kiini'yi koja Ejiogbe.

The Supporter, the Supporter, the Supporter. I beg you be with me that I may have honor, be with me that I may have respect, there is no Odu more honored and respected than the Supporter.

Ejiogbe ni Baba - gbogbo won.

The Supporter is the Father of all Odu.

Ki gbogbo eniyan kaakiri agbaye gbarajo, kiwon maa gbe'mi n'ija, kiegbe mi leke ota. Ki nle'ke odi.

Let all those in the world gather to help me, through my difficulties, to defeat my enemies. Raise me above all misfortune in my lifetime.

Kiemaa gbe'mi n'ija kiemaa gbe mi leke isoro lojo gbogbo no gbogbo ojo aye mi.

---

[138]Enrico Cerulli. The folk-literature of the Galla of Southern Abyssinia. p. 137. Public domain. Reprinted with permission from Seltzer Books.

Forever raise me above all misfortune that might come my way.
Kiemaa gbe ire ko mi nigbabogbo tabi kiemaagbe fun mi. Ase.
Always bring me good fortune. May it be so.[139]

32 - 1 Enoch[140] – Ethiopian (Jewish and Christian) Text

And in those days a whirlwind carried me off from the earth,
And set me down at the end of the heavens.

And there I saw another vision, the dwelling-places of the holy,
And the resting-places of the righteous.
Here mine eyes saw their dwellings with His righteous angels,
And their resting-places with the holy.

And they petitioned and interceded and prayed for the children of men,
And righteousness flowed before them as water,

And mercy like dew upon the earth:
Thus it is amongst them for ever and ever.

And in that place mine eyes saw the Elect One of righteousness and of faith,
And I saw his dwelling-place under the wings of the Lord of Spirits.
And righteousness shall prevail in his days,
And the righteous and elect shall be without number before Him for ever and ever.
And all the righteous and elect before Him shall be strong as fiery lights,
And their mouth shall be full of blessing,

---

[139] "African Traditional Religions." Reprinted with permission - Will Coleman, Ph.D. (Baba Esuyemi Ifayemi), Associate Professor at the Interdenominational Theological Center, and Awo Fa'lokun Fatunmbi, with assistance from Brad Ost, Head of Reference Services and Theological Librarian at the Atlanta University Center Robert W. Woodruff Library. https://research.auctr.edu/Ifa/Chap9Prayer

[140] 1 Enoch 39:1-14 excerpts (R.H. Charles 1912)
(https://archive.org/details/cu31924067146773/page/76/mode/2up).

And their lips extol the name of the Lord of Spirits,
And righteousness before Him shall never fail,
[And uprightness shall never fail before Him.]
There I wished to dwell,
And my spirit longed for that dwelling-place:

And there heretofore hath been my portion,
For so has it been established concerning me before the Lord of Spirits.

In those days I praised and extolled the name of the Lord of Spirits with blessings and praises, because He hath destined me for blessing and glory according to the good pleasure of the Lord of Spirits. For a long time my eyes regarded that place, and I blessed Him and praised Him, saying: "Blessed is He, and may He be blessed from the beginning and for evermore. And before Him there is no ceasing. He knows before the world was created what is for ever and what will be from generation unto generation. Those who sleep not bless Thee: they stand before Thy glory and bless, praise, and extol, saying: 'Holy, holy, holy, is the Lord of Spirits: He filleth the earth with spirits.'"

And here my eyes saw all those who sleep not: they stand before Him and bless and say: "Blessed be Thou, and blessed be the name of the Lord for ever and ever." And my face was changed; for I could no longer behold.

33 - End of the Age

In the Abrahamic Religions, you find the story about two of the children of Adam and Eve, brothers known as Cain and Abel. God had instructed them to make a sacrifice in a particular way as part of their worship and love for Him but Cain dishonored God's instructions. God expressed His acceptance of Abel's sacrifice but He expressed His displeasure with the disrespectful manner in which Cain offered the sacrifice and subsequently Cain became jealous of Abel and murdered his brother. As you can see the first murder that took place, according to this story, was committed misusing the name of God in religion.

The end of the age writings in some of the various religions can be seen in the context of family life: suppose you, as a parent, stepped out of a room in your home where your children were playing with one another and then you return to find them all fighting with one another, hurting each other and destroying your house. Every parent has had this experience. What is the first thing that you did? You may have raised your scary voice, broke up the fight, told them to stop talking, sit down, and then asked them to speak, one at a time. Then you instructed them each to seek forgiveness from the other, made sure they understood the unacceptableness of their behavior in hurting one another as well as hurting your house, apologized to one another, apologized to you, promised to never do it again and give each other a hug, give the parents a hug and then go outside and play. What usually follows is a lot of peace and joy. Imagine God as a parent, coming upon his children killing each other, hurting each other to the point of annihilation and destroying their home. What if God raised His "scary voice", put a stop to evil destruction, made sure that everyone listened to one another, admitted their wrongdoing, promised never to do it again, thereby preventing annihilation of our family and destruction of our home.

Imagine what that circumstance might look like.

What you commonly see in the scriptures of these various religions that speak about the end of the age are examples of increasing human depravity, an increase of greed, corruption and oppression from some of the rich and/or governments, shortened lifespans, corrupted spiritual leaders, corruption within family structure, notable cosmic events as well as the effects of evil human behavior on the planet.

To be sure, there are some incongruous aspects to each of these versions of the end of the age and I am not implying that everyone is saying the same thing, but only to look for what may enlighten, promote oneness and bring hope, seeking the Voice to light the way.

From the Abrahamic religions you find in the Jewish Tanakh prophecies related to end of the age in the books of Genesis, Daniel, Zechariah, and Isaiah, as well as others. From the Christian religion, you see prophecies related to the end of the age in the books of Matthew, Luke, Revelation, 1 Nephi 14, and in some of the letters. From Islam, you see references to the state of the world at the time of the end of the age in chapter 75 of **Surah Al-Qiyamah** (The Rising of the Dead and Resurrection). This passage discusses the state of humanity at the end of the age, signs in the cosmos and the importance of the only place of safety being with God ("with your Lord alone shall on that day, be the place of rest"). From the Bahai faith you can read about the end of the age from the book called the "World Order of Bahaullah" as well as the "Promised Day is Come". These are books written by Shoghi Effendi that talk about the end of the age and the importance of divine justice for the benefit of all.[141]

In the Indigenous faiths and traditions, notably the Native American Hopi Tradition, there are end of the age prophetic writings that emphasize how to survive the chaotic and catastrophic changes in both earth and in society through your spiritual practice.[142]

The Zoroastrian religious book of Denkard Book 7 (chapters 10 and 11) talks about aid for the faithful, coming from the heavenly realm, to help all deal with the earth's catastrophes at the end of the age.[143]

Buddhist literature contains an interesting story about King Pasenadi, a contemporary of the Buddha. He had a series of 16 dreams that frightened him, so he asked his friend, Buddha, to interpret them. The interpretation that followed from Buddha was that these dreams of

---

[141] https://ebible.org/engjps/index.htm

https://ebible.org/eng-asv/index.htm

https://www.gutenberg.org/cache/epub/7440/pg7440-images.html

https://bahai-library.com/writings/shoghieffendi/wob/woball.html

https://www.bahai.org/library/authoritative-texts/shoghi-effendi/promised-day-come/1#817131609

[142] https://sacred-texts.com/nam/hopi/toth/index.htm

and https://sacredland.org/hopi-prophecy/

[143] https://www.avesta.org/denkard/dk7.html#chap10

declining society and world chaos were prophetic in nature and were for the future end of the age and according to his interpretations, were some 2500 years away putting that at about the year 1957 of our current age. Buddha also predicted that the Dharma would decline as people will stop practicing it, resulting in moral decay over time.[144]

In Daoist teaching, there is a book known as the Thai-Shang - Tractate of Actions and Their Retributions. It talks about the cycles of life, and the consequences of human-made calamities.[145]

From Sikhism you can read about the Dark Age of the Kali Yuga in the Guru Granth Sahib Ji which tells of increasing evil, judgement by True God, the destruction of all that is evil and reinforces that the words of the True God stand.[146]

From the Hindu religion, you can read from the book "Srimad Bhagavatam – the Story of the Fortunate One" – Chapter 12, about the moral decay at the end of the age and that human righteousness is rescued by the return of Kalki, a manifestation of God, who comes from the heavenly realm and will subdue evil and rescue humanity.[147]

This is not an exhaustive list nor an academic version of end of the age spiritual literature but recommended reading from my friends from which I selected passages meaningful to me that I see as representative of the course of events and themes in the end of the age and as promoting oneness of humanity and the oneness of God.

As pointed out to me by my various friends in these religions, there is a cyclic nature to these described human events, not just linear. A unique way to look at this is from the ancient Hindu mathematicians who described the concept we call infinity and regarded the circle as an infinite number of straight lines. There is a similar understanding of cycles, or the circular nature of human progress, in the history of

---

[144] https://www.scribd.com/document/37467937/The-Sixteen-Dreams-of-King-Pasenadi-Kosala

[145] https://sacred-texts.com/tao/sbe40/sbe4018.htm

[146] https://archive.org/details/darshan_singh/darshan_singh/page/XXIII/mode/2up

[147] https://bhagavata.org/canto12/chapter2.html

humankind, across many religions. This concept helps me to see the world events as progressing in both linear and cyclical manner.

In verbiage from the scriptures such as in Christianity, one sees this underlying belief of "cyclical/ linear" events in the story about the creation with Adam and Eve instructed by God to "replenish" the earth, and the end of the age capped off by a tribulation, followed by a conquering of evil, the redemption of the Earth with resulting peace, no more death, and no more tears and all creation being "made new", that is to say not all new things but all things becoming new and directly inhabited and governed by True God.

For myself, I believe from my prayers that the common underlying and urgent point in all these writings is to refrain from evil and seek and follow Truth and Love in our "inner kingdom" (where you can hear the Voice and seek and follow the path the Voice lights up), consistently considered as "one" in existence among these religions.

PASSAGES ON THE END OF THE AGE FROM VARIOUS RELIGIONS:

Hinduism:

Srimad Bhagavatam excerpts from Chapter 12 The Story of the Fortunate One

When the bodies of all living entities are in decay from the contamination of Kali-yuga, when the dutifulness of the members of all status-orientations is lost, when the Vedic path for all man has changed into a predominantly atheistic sense of duty, when the kings [or governors] mainly consist of thieves, and the people in their various occupations are lying criminals of useless violence [against specially animals], when the societal classes as good as all are engaged in profit-minded labor, cows have the same value as goats, the hermitages hardly can be distinguished from materialistic households, family bonds do not reach beyond the ties of marriage, when the plants and herbs are mostly small sized and all trees are like s'amî trees, when there is always lightning in the clouds and the homes are ruled by loneliness [voidism and impersonalism, see Pranâti], when Kali-yuga is running at its end and the people behave like asses, the Supreme Lord will descend in the mode of pure goodness to defend the dharma.

The spiritual master of all the moving and nonmoving living beings, Lord Vishnu, the Supreme Personality and Controller of All, takes birth for the protection of the religion and to put an end to the karma of the saintly souls... After the Supreme Lord Kalki, the Lord and Master of Dharma, has incarnated, Satya-yuga will begin and progeny will be created in the mode of goodness.[148]

Islam

IN THE NAME OF THE MOST MERCIFUL GOD.
VERILY I swear by the day of resurrection;
and I swear by the soul which accuseth itself:
doth man think that we will not gather his bones together?
Yea: we are able to put together the smallest bones of his fingers.
But man chooseth to be wicked, for the time which is before him.
He asketh, When will the day of resurrection be?
But when the sight shall be dazzled,
and the moon shall be eclipsed,
and the sun and the moon shall be in conjunction;
on that day man shall say, Where is a place of refuge?
By no means: there shall be no place to fly unto.
With thy LORD shall be the sure mansion of rest on that day:
on that day shall a man be told that which he hath done first and last.
Yea; a man shall be an evidence against himself:
and though he offer his excuses, they shall not be received.
Move not thy tongue, O Mohammed, in repeating the revelations brought

---

[148] https://bhagavata.org/canto12/chapter2.html

thee by Gabriel, before he shall have finished the same, that thou
mayest quickly commit them to memory:

for the collecting the Koran in thy mind, and the teaching thee the
true reading thereof, are incumbent on us.

But when we shall have read the same unto thee by the tongue of the
angel, do thou follow the reading thereof:

and afterwards it shall be our part to explain it unto thee.

By no means shalt thou be thus hasty for the future. But ye love that
which hasteneth away,

and neglect the life to come.

Some countenances on that day shall be bright,

looking towards their LORD:

and some countenances, on that day, shall be dismal:

they shall think that a crushing calamity shall be brought upon them.

Assuredly. When a man's soul shall come up to his throat, in his last
agony, and the standers-by shall say, Who bringeth a charm to
recover him?

and shall think it to be his departure out of this world.

Quran – Surah 75 – the Resurrection; revealed at Mecca[149]

Zoroastrianism

*Concerning the marvellousness of Soshyant (one who brings benefit; a
deliverer or savior) as to the splendour and glory of person, it says that "when
the coming of the last Soshyant is born whose food is spiritual and body
sunny (that is his body is as radiant as the sun)" ; also this, that "he looks
on all sides with six-eyed power and sees the remedy for persecution by the
fiend." And all mankind remain of one accord in the religion of Ohrmazd
(aka Ahura Mazda, the Wise Lord, Supreme Creator), owing to the will of
the creator, the command of that apostle, and the resources of his
companions. At the end of the fifty seven years the fiend and Ahriman (evil
destructive spirit) are annihilated, the renovation for the future existence
occurs, and the whole of the good creation is provided with purity and*

---

[149] https://www.gutenberg.org/cache/epub/7440/pg7440-images.html

perfect splendour. Then those Mazda (Supreme God) worshippers produce a longing for the renovation among the existences, one ever-living, ever-beneficial, and ever desiring a Lord. "Then I, who am Ohrmazd (Supreme Creator), produce the renovation according to the longing among the existences, one ever-living, ever-beneficial, and ever desiring a lord".

Denkard Book 7 Excerpts from Chapter 11. Soshyant and the Renovation [Frashegird].[150]

Buddhism

Excerpts from the Mahasupina Jataka – Chapter 77 – on the interpretation of the sixteen dreams of King Pasenadi as told to Buddha regarding the end of the age and the interpretation thereof. These were interpreted by Buddha as applying to a time approximately 2500 years from when this dream interpretation occurred (which would be approximately our current time year of 1957)

"Bulls first, and trees."—This story was told by the Master while at Jetavana about sixteen wonderful dreams. For in the last watch of one night (so tradition says) the King of Kosala (named King Pasenadi), who had been asleep all the night, dreamed sixteen great dreams, and woke up in great fright and alarm as to what they might portend for him. So strong was the fear of death upon him that he could not stir, but lay there huddled up on his bed. Now, when the night grew light, his brahmins and chaplains came to him and with due obeisance asked whether his majesty had slept well.

"How could I sleep well, my directors?" answered the king. "For just at daybreak I dreamed sixteen wonderful dreams, and I have been in terror ever since! Tell me, my directors, what it all means."

"We shall be able to judge, on hearing them."

Then the king told them his dreams, and asked what those visions would entail upon him.

The brahmins fell a-wringing their hands! "Why wring your hands,

---

[150] https://www.avesta.org/denkard/dk7.html#chap10

brahmins?" asked the king. "Because, sire, these are evil dreams." "What will come of them?" said the king. "One of three calamities,—harm to your kingdom, to your life, or to your riches." "Is there a remedy, or is there not?" "Undoubtedly these dreams in themselves are so threatening as to be without remedy; but none the less we will find a remedy for them.

"My directors," cried the king in his terror, "my life is in your hands; make haste and work my safety." "Large sums of money, and large supplies of food of every kind will be ours," thought the exultant brahmins;

Now their doings were watched by Queen Mallika, who came to the king and asked what made these brahmins keep coming to him.

"I envy you," said the king; "a snake in your ear, and you not to know of it!" "What does your majesty mean?" "I have dreamed, oh such unlucky dreams! The brahmins tell me they point to one of three calamities; and they are anxious to offer sacrifices to avert the evil. And this is what brings them here so often." "But has your majesty consulted the Chief Brahmin (Buddha) both of this world and of the world of devas?" "Who, pray, may he be, my dear?" asked the king. "Know you not that chiefest personage of all the world, the all-knowing and pure, the spotless master-brahmin? Surely, he, the Blessed One (Buddha), will understand your dreams. Go, ask him." "And so I will, my queen," said the king. And away he went to the monastery, saluted the Master, and sat down.....

Buddha: "Tell me your ninth dream."

The king: "Methought, sir, I saw a deep pool with shelving banks all round and over-grown with the five kinds of lotuses. From every side two-footed creatures and four-footed creatures flocked thither to drink of its waters. The depths in the middle were muddy, but the water was clear and sparkling at the margin where the various creatures went down into the pool. This was my ninth dream. What shall come of it?"

Buddha: "This dream too shall not have its fulfilment till the future. For in days to come kings shall grow unrighteous; they shall rule after their own will and pleasure, and shall not execute judgment according to righteousness. These kings shall hunger after riches and wax fat on bribes; they shall not shew mercy, love and compassion toward their people, but be fierce and cruel, amassing wealth by crushing their subjects like sugar-canes in a mill and by taxing them even to the uttermost farthing. Unable to pay the oppressive tax, the people shall fly from village and town and the like, and take refuge upon the borders of the realm; the heart of the land shall be a wilderness, while the borders shall teem with people,—even as the water was muddy in the middle of the pool and clear at the margin. Howbeit, you have nothing to fear therefrom. Tell me your tenth dream.".....

Tell me your sixteenth dream."

"Heretofore, sir, it always used to be panthers that preyed on goats; but methought I saw goats chasing panthers and devouring them—munch, munch, munch!—whilst at bare sight of the goats afar off, terror-stricken wolves fled quaking with fear and hid themselves in their fastnesses in the thicket. Such was my dream. What shall come of it?"

"This dream too shall not have its fulfilment till the future, till the reign of unrighteous kings. In those days the low-born shall be raised to lordship and be made royal favourites, whilst the nobles shall sink into obscurity and distress. Gaining influence in the courts of law because of their favour with the king, these upstarts shall claim perforce the ancestral estates, the raiment, and all the property of the old nobility. And-when these latter plead their rights before the courts, then shall the king's minions have them cudgelled and bastinadoed and taken by the throat and cast out with words of scorn, such as—'Know your place, fools! What? do you dispute with us? The king shall know of your insolence, and we will have your hands and feet chopped off and other correctives applied!' Hereupon the terrified nobles shall affirm that their own belongings really belong to the overbearing upstarts, and will tell the favourites to accept them. And they shall hie them home and there cower in an agony of fear. Likewise, evil Brethren shall harry at pleasure good and worthy Brethren, till these latter, finding none to help them, shall flee to the jungle. And this oppression of the nobles and of the good Brethren by the low-born and by the evil brethren, shall be like the scaring of wolves by goats. Howbeit, you have nothing to fear therefrom. For this dream too has reference to future times only. It was not truth, it was not love for you, that prompted the brahmins to prophesy as they did. No, it was greed of gain, and the insight that is bred of covetousness, that shaped all their self-seeking utterances."

Thus did the Master expound the import of these sixteen great dreams, adding,—"You, sire, are not the first to have these dreams; they were dreamed by kings of bygone days also; and, then as now, the brahmins found in them a pretext for sacrifices; whereupon, at the instance of the wise and good, the Bodhisatta was consulted, and the dreams were expounded by them of old time in just the same manner as they have now been expounded.

Public domain copy of Stories of the Buddha's Former Births Book 1 Ekanipāta 77. Mahasupina Jātaka. "[151]

Sikhism

Writings of Guru Nanak on all returning to the One Imperishable God in the end: Page 1100

Nanak says, "Those eyes are different, which can see my Master."
Nanak says, "There are very few, who have true in their mind."
My Dear's face is beautiful, I see Him day and night.
I saw my Master in sleep, I sacrifice myself for that dream
the true Master in mind, do not speak stupid from {your} mouth.
See in your mind, Dear is not away from you.
The earth, the sky, the nether regions, the moon, the sun, all are perishable.
The poor in humility and the rich in ego, all will leave the world.
The Kazi, the Sheikh, the Sheikhs, all will stand and go.
The Peers, the prophets, the men of God, none will remain stable.
The fasts, the call for prayer, the prayer, all will go without realizing.
The eighty four lacs of beings, all come and go.

Stable is true God, man of one God becomes imperishable.
I have tried and searched everywhere, there is none other than One.

Whatever is seen, will perish, everything is perishable, shall perish.
Only supreme God is ever-living, and His servant shall live.

---

[151] https://suttacentral.net/ja77/en/chalmers?lang=en&reference=none&highlight=false

You yearn for One, and realize only One.

Excerpts From the Guru Granth Sahib Ji – Page 1100[152]

Judaism

And at that time shall Michael (Archangel) stand up, the great prince who standeth for the children of thy people; and there shall be a time of trouble, such as never was since there was a nation even to that same time; and at that time thy people shall be delivered, every one that shall be found written in the book. 2 And many of them that sleep in the dust of the earth shall awake, some to everlasting life, and some to reproaches and everlasting abhorrence. 3 And they that are wise shall shine as the brightness of the firmament; and they that turn the many to righteousness as the stars for ever and ever. 4 But thou, O Daniel, shut up the words, and seal the book, even to the time of the end; many shall run to and fro, and knowledge shall be increased.' 5 Then I Daniel looked, and, behold, there stood other two, the one on the bank of the river on this side, and the other on the bank of the river on that side. 6 And one said to the man clothed in linen, who was above the waters of the river: 'How long shall it be to the end of the wonders?' 7 And I heard the man clothed in linen, who was above the waters of the river, when he lifted up his right hand and his left hand unto heaven, and swore by Him that liveth for ever that it shall be for a time, times, and a half; and when they have made an end of breaking in pieces the power of the holy people, all these things shall be finished. 8 And I heard, but I understood not; then said I: 'O my Lord, what shall be the latter end of these things?' 9 And he said: 'Go thy way, Daniel; for the words are shut up and sealed till the time of the end. 10 Many shall purify themselves, and make themselves white, and be refined; but the wicked shall do wickedly; and none of the wicked shall understand; but they that are wise shall understand. 11 And from the time that the continual burnt-offering shall be taken away, and the detestable thing that causes appalment (abominable desecration) set up, there shall be a

---

[152]https://archive.org/details/darshan_singh/darshan_singh/page/2321/mode/2up
public domain

thousand two hundred and ninety days. 12 Happy is he that waiteth, and cometh to the thousand three hundred and five and thirty days. 13 But go thou thy way till the end be; and thou shalt rest, and shalt stand up to thy lot, at the end of the days.

Excerpts from the Jewish Tanakh -Book of Daniel Chapter 12[153]

For, behold, I create new heavens and a new earth; and the former things shall not be remembered, nor come into mind.

Isaiah 65:17 Jewish Tanakh [154]

Christianity

And as Jesus sat on the mount of Olives, his disciples came, and said

between themselves and him: Tell us when these things are to be; and what will be the sign of your coming, and of the end of the age. Jesus answered and said to them: Take heed, that no one deceive you. For nation will rise against nation, and kingdom against kingdom; and there will be famines, and pestilences, and earthquakes in diverse places. But all these are only the commencement of sorrows. And they will deliver you up to tribulation, and will kill you: and you will

be hated by all nations, on account of my name. And on account of the abounding of iniquity, the love of many will decline. But he that shall persevere to the end, will have life. And this announcement of the kingdom shall be published in all the world, for a testimony to all nations: and then will come the consummation (the end).

And when you see the abominable sign of desolation, which was spoken of by Daniel the prophet ("And from the time that the continual burnt-offering shall be taken away, and the detestable thing that causes appalment set up...", Daniel 12:11), standing in the holy place; then let the reader consider; and then let them who are in Judaea, flee to the mountain: For there will then be great distress, such as has not been from the commencement of the world, until now, and will not be. And unless those days should be cut

---

[153] https://ebible.org/engjps/DAN12.htm

[154] https://ebible.org/engjps/ISA65.htm

short, no flesh would remain alive. But, for the elect's sake, those days will be cut short. As the lightning comes out of the east, and shines unto the west, so will be the coming of the Son of man. And immediately after the distress of those days, the sun will be darkened, and the moon will not show her light, and the stars will fall from heaven, and the powers of heaven will be agitated. And then will be seen the signal of the Son of man in heaven: and then will all the tribes of the earth mourn, when they see the Son of man coming on the clouds of heaven, with power and great glory. And he will send his angels with a great trumpet and they will collect together his elect from the four winds, from one extremity of heaven to the other. Watch, therefore, since you know not at what hour your Lord comes. Therefore, you also be ready; for at an hour you do not expect, the Son of man will come.
Excerpts from Matthew Chapter 24

And when these things shall begin to be, take courage, and lift up your heads, for your deliverance draws near.
Luke 21:28

And I saw heaven opened: and lo, a white horse; and he that sat on it, is
called Faithful and True: and in righteousness he judges, and makes war.
His eyes were like a flame of fire, and on his head were many diadems;
and he had names inscribed; and the name which was written on him, no one knew, except himself. And he was clothed with a vesture sprinkled with blood; and his name is called, The Word of God. And the soldiery of heaven followed him, on white horses, clad in garments of fine linen, pure and white. And from his mouth issued a sharp two-edged sword, that with it he could smite the nations; and he will rule the nations with a rod of iron; and he will tread the wine-press of the wrath of God Almighty. And he has upon his vesture and upon his thigh the words written: King of kings, and Lord of lords.
Excerpts from the Book of Revelation - Chapter 19

And I saw new heavens, and a new earth: for the former heaven and the former earth had passed away: and the sea was no more....

Behold, the tabernacle of God is with men, and he shall dwell with them, and they shall be his peoples, and God himself shall be with them, and be their God: 4 and he shall wipe away every tear from their eyes; and death shall be no more; neither shall there be mourning, nor crying, nor pain, any more: the first things are passed away. 5 And he that sits on the throne said, Behold, I make all things new. And he said, Write: for these words are faithful and true.

Excerpts from the Book of Revelation Chapter 21[155]

---

[155] Excerpts from the public domain English translation of the Syriac Peshito (Aramaic) Version of the New Testament Bible, translated by Murdock in 1852 with modernized English

WISDOM

CHAPTER 4

THE TWELVE PRINCIPLES OF ONENESS™

In 2001, after a lengthy prayer retreat, I was traveling on a flight to Africa for our foundation. I was sleeping soundly, when somewhere over the Atlantic Ocean, the Voice suddenly woke me up and told me forcefully to "write these words down!" What those words turned out to be are the Twelve Principles for living in Oneness. I have found these principles to be acceptable to most people of most faiths and religions I have spoken to. People have told me that these principles have answered the question of: "Ok, I believe in True One God (or Consciousness)—now what?"

Ask yourself if practicing these twelve principles will cause you any harm. Adopt what you can of what you find acceptable. Live by these principles and see if your life is better—if you and your family are happier. Any one of these twelve can serve as your focus for meditation. Practice as often as you can.

With each of the twelve principles I have placed references from various religions that have corresponding scriptures or doctrine. There are so many such examples that, for practical purposes, I have limited the references to just a few, but you are welcome to explore many more.

TWELVE PRINCIPLES OF ONENESS™ [156]

1. **Love, worship and honor God** with praise, obedience, sacrifice, humility, and seeking forgiveness. Place God first in every thought, word, and action.

2. **God is almighty, present all over, all knowing and most gracious.** Experiencing God beyond any physical shape or earthly object is vital. Do not use God's name for selfish or unrighteous purposes.

3. **Love and honor parents** with care all their lives, in obedience and respect.

4. **Love and honor, with respect and humility, the ones who teach you righteousness**—and what they teach you.

5. **Love your family** with humility, time and cheer—taking care of them, encouraging them to lead a closer walk with God, and setting an example.

6. **Love your neighbors**, forgiving their wrongdoings and showing greater care for your neighbors' possessions and life than you would for your own.

7. **Love the poor, sick, old, weak, handicapped, orphans, widows, lonely, abused, outcasts and downtrodden** with compassion—giving them what they need as much as you can.

8. **Stay away from envy, greed, self-centered pride, anger, gluttony, lust (unrighteous desire), sloth (laziness) and unrighteous attachments**—to refrain from the temptation of evil.

9. **Respect and learn good in others' ways and beliefs**, enabling them to learn good from your faith and works more than from your words.

---

[156] Copyright Ramanjaneyulu Tanguturi 2001. Received by Ramanjaneyulu (Rom) Tanguturi in 2001 on the way to Africa after a time of fasting, prayers and meditation in solitude. These principles are a guide to living various aspects of day-to-day life in a godly way, acceptable to most faiths, religions, and humanity, and are meant to promote and bring peace and joy through oneness of humanity with the one God and worshipping in oneness with love.

10. **Maintain your body with care**, as the soul given by God lives in it, and **preserve and respect nature and all the creation of God**, selectively utilizing resources for righteous purposes.

11. **Spend one day a week** in worship, spiritual enrichment, enhancement of family togetherness and physical rest, meeting only the needs you must and fasting as led in your prayers.

12. **Pray without ceasing** for oneness, peace, and joy for all, asking God to help you do God's will, to reach God, the Ultimate, and to attain Oneness with God.

CORRESPONDING SCRIPTURES AND WRITINGS FROM MULTIPLE RELIGIONS:

1. Love, worship and honor God with praise, obedience, sacrifice, humility, and seeking forgiveness. Place God first in every thought, word, and action.

Christianity: *Jesus said to him, "You shall love the Lord your God with all your heart, with all your soul, and with all your mind."*[157]

For I know that God is not a partial God, neither a changeable being; but he is unchangeable from all eternity to all eternity.[158]

Confucianism: *To put the world in order, we must first put the nation in order; to put the nation in order, we must first put the family in order; to put the family in order; we must first cultivate our personal life; we must first set our hearts right.*[159]

---

[157] Matthew 22:37 (WEB).

[158] Book of Mormon - Moroni Chapter 8:18
https://www.gutenberg.org/cache/epub/17/pg17-images.html#link2H_4_0015

[159] Legge, James (trans.) Confucius: Confucian Analects, The Great Learning and The Doctrine of the Mean (Dover 1971).

Zoroastrianism:
Excerpts from Yasna XXXIV:

As to those (three gifts of blessings), Immor-
tality, the Righteous Order and the (established)
Kingdom of Welfare, which Thou, O Mazda! hast
given through (holy) deeds, words, and the sacrifice
unto these (Thy servants here in my sight), gifts
(shall) be offered by us in return to Thee, O Ahura
and with the foremost of them all;

Yea, and all those gifts of the Good Spirit
have been given (back in gratitude) to Thee by the
mind and the deed of the bountiful man, whose soul
goes hand in hand with the Righteous Order in
the settlement, in homage toward the One like You;

What is then Your Kingdom, O Mazda?
What are Your riches? that I may become Your
own in my actions, with the Righteous Order, and
(Thy) Good Mind, to care for Your poor (in their
Suffering).

Which (of what kind) is your sovereignty? (that is, what thing can I do,
whereby your sovereignty may be increased through my instrumentality?)
And
which is your wealth? (that is, what thing shall I do whereby
riches may be kept in your possession by my means?) How thus-
in the actions of Ahura Mazda shall I become yours?

If thus Ye are in verity, O Mazda! with the
Righteous Order and Thy Good Mind, then grant
Ye me a sign of this in this world's entire abiding
(while I live amid its scenes), how offering sacrifice

and praising You the more devoutly
I may approach You (in my worship)
I know none other than You; then do Ye save us through Your
Righteousness;

Teach Thou us the paths through Righteousness,
those verily trod by (Thy) Good Mind, (as He lives
within Thy saints. [160]

Hinduism: *Have Me, then, in thy heart always! and fight!*
Thou too, when heart and mind are fixed on Me,
Shalt surely come to Me! All come who cleave
With never-wavering will of firmest faith,
Owning none other Gods: all come to Me,
The Uttermost, Purusha, Holiest! [161]

2. God is almighty, present all over, all knowing and most gracious.

Experiencing God beyond any physical shape or earthly object is vital.
Do not use God's name for selfish or unrighteous purposes.

Hinduism: *That way--the highest way--goes he who shuts*
The gates of all his senses, locks desire
Safe in his heart, centres the vital airs
Upon his parting thought, steadfastly set;
And, murmuring OM, the sacred syllable--
Emblem of BRAHM--dies, meditating Me.
For who, none other Gods regarding, looks
Ever to Me, easily am I gained
By such a Yogi; and, attaining Me,
They fall not--those Mahatmas--back to birth,

---

[160] Sacred Books of the East; the Zend Avesta; translated by L. H. Mills 1887
https://ia600800.us.archive.org/1/items/in.ernet.dli.2015.495279/2015.495279.THA-SACRED_text.pdf

[161] https://www.gutenberg.org/files/2388/2388-h/2388-h.htm#chap08 trans. Arnold

To life, which is the place of pain, which ends,
But take the way of utmost blessedness.[162]

Islam: *Nothing is hidden from Allah, whether on Earth or in Heaven.*[163]

Taoism:

> *25*
> *Before the universe was born*
> *there was something in the chaos of the heavens.*
> *It stands alone and empty,*
> *solitary and unchanging.*
> *It is ever present and secure.*
> *It may be regarded as the Mother of the universe.*
> *Because I do not know its name, I call it the Tao.*
> *If forced to give it a name,*
> *I would call it 'Great'.*
> *Because it is Great means it is everywhere. Being everywhere means it is eternal.*
> *Being eternal means everything returns to it.*
> *Tao is great.*
> *Heaven is great.*
> *Earth is great.*
> *Humanity is great.*
> *Within the universe, these are the four great things.*
> *Humanity follows the earth. Earth follows Heaven. Heaven follows the Tao. The Tao follows only itself.*[164]

3. Love and honor parents with care all their lives, in obedience and respect.

---

[162] https://www.gutenberg.org/files/2388/2388-h/2388-h.htm#chap08 trans. Arnold

[163] Qur'an 14:38 (trans. Yusuf).

[164] *Tao Te Ching* 25 (trans. JH McDonald 1996 for Public Domain).

Judaism: *Honour thy father and thy mother, in that thy days may be long upon the land which the LORD, thy God, giveth thee.*[165]

Hinduism: *Be one to whom a mother is as god, be one to whom a father is as god,*

Be one to whom an Acharya (spiritual guide, scholars you learn from) is as god, be one to whom a guest is as god.

Let your actions be uncensurable, none else.

Those acts that you consider good when done to you, do those to others, none else.[166]

Islam: *Thy Lord hath decreed that ye worship none but Him, and that ye be kind to parents. Whether one or both of them attain old age in thy life, say not to them a word of contempt, nor repel them, but address them in terms of honour.*

And, out of kindness, lower to them the wing of humility, and say: "My Lord! bestow on them thy Mercy even as they cherished me in childhood."[167]

4. <u>Love and honor, with respect and humility, the ones who teach you righteousness</u> and what they teach you.

Christianity: *Therefore I urge you, brothers, by the mercies of God, to present your bodies a living sacrifice, holy, acceptable to God, which is your spiritual service. 2 Don't be conformed to this world, but be transformed by the renewing of your mind, so that you may prove what is the good, well-pleasing, and perfect will of God.*

---

[165] https://ebible.org/engjps/EXO20.htm JPS Tanakh 1917
[166] Taittriya Upanishad 1:11:2 (trans. Muller).
[167] Qur'an 117:23-24 (trans. Yusuf).

3 For I say through the grace that was given me, to everyone who is among you, not to think of yourself more highly than you ought to think; but to think reasonably, as God has apportioned to each person a measure of faith. 4 For even as we have many members in one body, and all the members don't have the same function, 5 so we, who are many, are one body in Christ, and individually members of one another, 6 having gifts differing according to the grace that was given to us: if prophecy, let's prophesy according to the proportion of our faith; 7 or service, let's give ourselves to service; or he who teaches, to his teaching; 8 or he who exhorts, to his exhorting; he who gives, let him do it with generosity; he who rules, with diligence; he who shows mercy, with cheerfulness.[168]

Bahai Faith: *That the diverse communions of the earth, and the manifold systems of religious belief, should never be allowed to foster the feelings of animosity among men, is, in this Day, of the essence of the Faith of God and His Religion. These principles and laws, these firmly-established and mighty systems, have proceeded from one Source, and are rays of one Light. That they differ one from another is to be attributed to the varying requirements of the ages in which they were promulgated.*[169]

5. <u>Love your family</u> with humility, time and cheer—taking care of them, encouraging them to lead a closer walk with God, and setting an example.

Judaism: *Therefore a man shall leave his father and mother and be joined to his wife, and they shall become one flesh.*[170]

As a father pities his children, So the Lord pities those who fear Him.

---

[168] Romans 12:4-8 (WEB).

[169] Epistle to the Son of the Wolf by Mírzá Ḥusayn-'Alí Núrí known as Bahá'u'lláh **https://www.gutenberg.org/cache/epub/16697/pg16697-images.html** Printed with permission from Bahai.org

[170] Genesis 2:24.

For He knows our frame; He remembers that we are dust.[171]

Confucianism: *The Noble-minded cultivate roots. When roots are secure, the Way is born. To honor parents and elders – isn't that the root of Humanity?*[172]

Christianity: *And be kind to one another, tenderhearted, forgiving one another, even as God in Christ forgave you.*[173]

6. <u>Love your neighbors</u>, forgiving their wrongdoings and showing greater care for the neighbors' possessions and life than you would for your own.

Judaism: *13 Thou shalt not murder. 14 Thou shalt not commit adultery. 15 Thou shalt not steal. 16 Thou shalt not bear false witness against thy neighbour. 17 Thou shalt not covet thy neighbour's house; thou shalt not covet thy neighbour's wife, nor his man-servant, nor his maid-servant, nor his ox, nor his ass, nor any thing that is thy neighbour's.*[174]

10 Have we not all one father? Hath not one God created us? Why do we deal treacherously every man against his brother, profaning the covenant of our fathers?[175]

Buddhism: *For hatred does not cease by hatred at any time: hatred ceases by love, this is an old rule.*[176]

Atheism: *Treat others like you want to be treated.*

7. <u>Love the poor, sick, old, weak, handicapped, orphans, widows,</u>

---

[171] Psalms 103:13.

[172] The Analects of Confucius Chapter I.2.

[173] Ephesians 4:32.

[174] Exodus 20 (JPS Tanakh 1917).

[175] Malachi 2:10 (JPS Tanakh 1917).

[176] https://www.gutenberg.org/cache/epub/2017/pg2017-images.html#link2HCH0006

lonely, abused, outcasts and downtrodden with compassion—giving them what they need as much as you can.

Islam: *And those who believed and did righteous deeds will be admitted to gardens beneath which rivers flow, abiding eternally therein by permission of their Lord; and their greeting therein will be, "Peace!"*[177]

Christianity: *5 Listen, my beloved brothers. Didn't God choose those who are poor in this world to be rich in faith and heirs of the Kingdom which he promised to those who love him?*[178]

Atheism: *Service and endurance are the chief personal duties of Man. Secularism holds it to be the duty of every man to reserve a portion of his means and energies for the public service, and so to cultivate and cherish his powers, mental and physical, as to have them ever ready to perform service, as efficient as possible, to the well-being of humanity. No weakness, no passion, no wavering, should be found among those who are battling for the cause of human welfare, which such errors may fatally endure. Self-control, self-culture, self-sacrifice, are all essential to those who would serve that cause, and would not bring discredit upon their comrades in that service.*[179]

8. Stay away from envy, greed, self-centered pride, anger, gluttony, lust (unrighteous desire), sloth (laziness) and unrighteous attachments—to refrain from the temptation of evil.

Stoicism:[180] *Letter 14: We must follow the old adage and avoid three things with special care: hatred, jealousy, and scorn. And wisdom alone can show*

---

[177] Qur'an 14:23 (trans. Muhammed).

[178] James 2:5 (WEB).

[179] Excerpts from "the Principles of Secularism" by George Jacob Holyoake Chapter 5 https://www.gutenberg.org/cache/epub/36797/pg36797-images.html

[180] Excerpts from Moral Letters to Lucilius by Seneca. (https://en.wikisource.org/wiki/Moral_letters_to_Lucilius/Letter_41).

you how this may be done…Let us withdraw ourselves in every way; for it is as harmful to be scorned as to be admired.

Letter 39: It is the quality of a great soul to scorn great things and to prefer that which is ordinary rather than that which is too great. For the one condition is useful and life-giving; but the other does harm just because it is excessive. Similarly, too rich a soil makes the grain fall flat, branches break down under too heavy a load, excessive productiveness does not bring fruit to ripeness. This is the case with the soul also; for it is ruined by uncontrolled prosperity, which is used not only to the detriment of others, but also to the detriment of itself. Utility measures our needs; but by what standard can you check the superfluous? It is for this reason that men sink themselves in pleasures, and they cannot do without them when once they have become accustomed to them, and for this reason they are most wretched, because they have reached such a pass that what was once superfluous to them has become indispensable. And so they are the slaves of their pleasures instead of enjoying them; they even love their own ills and that is the worst ill of all! Then it is that the height of unhappiness is reached, when men are not only attracted, but even pleased, by shameful things, and when there is no longer any room for a cure, now that those things which once were vices have become habits. Farewell.

Christianity: *22 But the fruit of the Spirit is love, joy, peace, patience, kindness, goodness, faith, 23 gentleness, and self-control. Against such things there is no law.[181]*

Go your way, sell whatever you have and give to the poor, and you will have treasure in heaven; and come, take up the cross, and follow Me.[182]

Hinduism: *Fearlessness, singleness of soul, the will*
Always to strive for wisdom; opened hand
And governed appetites; and piety,
And love of lonely study; humbleness,

---

[181] Galatians 5: 22-23 (WEB).
[182] Mark 10:17-31.

Uprightness, heed to injure nought which lives,
Truthfulness, slowness unto wrath, a mind
That lightly letteth go what others prize;
And equanimity, and charity
Which spieth no man's faults; and tenderness
Towards all that suffer; a contented heart,
Fluttered by no desires; a bearing mild,
Modest, and grave, with manhood nobly mixed,
With patience, fortitude, and purity;
An unrevengeful spirit, never given
To rate itself too high;--such be the signs,
O Indian Prince! of him whose feet are set
On that fair path which leads to heavenly birth!
Deceitfulness, and arrogance, and pride,
Quickness to anger, harsh and evil speech,
And ignorance, to its own darkness blind,--
These be the signs, My Prince! of him whose birth
Is fated for the regions of the vile.[183]

9. <u>Respect and learn good in others' ways and beliefs</u>, enabling them to learn good from your faith and works more than from your words.
Buddhism:
Asoka, the Buddhist emperor of India – Excerpts from his "Rock Edicts XII"
    His Sacred and Gracious Majesty the King (Asoka) does reverence to men of all sects (religions), whether ascetics or householders, by gifts and various forms of reverence.
    His Sacred Majesty (Asoka), however, cares not so much for gifts or external reverence as that there should be a growth of the essence of the matter in all sects (religions). Depreciation (of religion) should be for specific reasons only, because the sects (religion) of other people all deserve reverence for one reason or another. By thus acting a man exalts his own sect (religion), and at the same time does service to the sects (religions) of other

---

[183] https://www.gutenberg.org/cache/epub/2388/pg2388-images.html#chap08

people. By acting contrariwise, a man hurts his own sect (religion) and does disservice to the sects (religions) of other people. For he who does reverence to his own sect (religion) while disparaging the sects (religions) of others wholly from attachment to his own, with intent to enhance the splendour of his own sect (religion), in reality by such conduct inflicts the severest injury on his own sect (religion).[184]

Christianity: *22 Paul stood in the middle of the Areopagus and said, "You men of Athens, I perceive that you are very religious in all things. 23 For as I passed along and observed the objects of your worship, I also found an altar with this inscription: 'TO AN UNKNOWN GOD.' What therefore you worship in ignorance, I announce to you. 24 The God who made the world and all things in it, he, being Lord of heaven and earth, doesn't dwell in temples made with hands.* [185]

10. **Maintain your body with care**, as the soul given by God lives in it, and **preserve and respect nature and all the creation of God**, selectively utilizing the resources for righteous purposes.

Judaism: *31 And God saw every thing that He had made, and, behold, it was very good. And there was evening and there was morning, the sixth day.* [186]

Christianity: *19 Or don't you know that your body is a temple of the Holy Spirit who is in you, whom you have from God? You are not your own, 20 for you were bought with a price. Therefore glorify God in your body and in your spirit, which are God's.* [187]

Islam: Quran Chapter LV - THE MERCIFUL; REVEALED AT MECCA

IN THE NAME OF THE MOST MERCIFUL GOD.

---

[184]Smith, Vincent, Asoka, the Buddhist Emperor of India, 1920, Page 149 .

[185] Acts 17:22-24 (WEB).

[186] Genesis 1:31 (JPS Tanakh 1917).

[187] 1 Corinthians 6:19 (WEB).

"THE Merciful hath taught his servant the Koran.

He created man:

he hath taught him distinct speech.

The sun and the moon run their courses according to a certain rule:

and the vegetables which creep on the ground, and the trees submit to his disposition.

He also raised the heaven; and he appointed the balance,

that ye should not transgress in respect to the balance:

wherefore observe a just weight; and diminish not the balance.

And the earth hath he prepared for living creatures:

therein are various fruits, and palm-trees bearing sheaths of flowers;

and grain having chaff, and leaves.

Which, therefore, of your LORD'S benefits will ye ungratefully deny?"[188]

11. <u>**Spend one day a week in worship**</u>, spiritual enrichment, enhancement of family togetherness and physical rest, meeting only the needs you must and fasting as led in your prayers.

Judaism: *8 Remember the sabbath day, to keep it holy. 9 Six days shalt thou labour, and do all thy work; 10 but the seventh day is a sabbath unto the LORD thy God, in it thou shalt not do any manner of work, thou, nor thy son, nor thy daughter, nor thy man-servant, nor thy maid-servant, nor thy cattle, nor thy stranger that is within thy gates; 11 for in six days the LORD made heaven and earth, the sea, and all that in them is, and rested on the seventh day; wherefore the LORD blessed the sabbath day, and hallowed it.*[189]

Christianity: *But you, when you fast, anoint your head and wash your face, 18 so that you are not seen by men to be fasting, but by your Father who is in secret; and your Father, who sees in secret, will reward you.*[190]

---

[188] https://www.gutenberg.org/cache/epub/7440/pg7440-images.html trans Sale

[189] Exodus 20:8-11 (JPS Tanakh 1917).

[190] Matthew 6:17 (WEB).

12. **Pray without ceasing** for oneness, peace, and joy for all, asking God to help you do God's will and to reach God, the Ultimate, and to attain Oneness with God.

Tenrikyo:

Looking all over the world and through all ages,
I find no one who has understood My heart.
So should it be, for I have never taught it before,
It is natural that you know nothing.
This time I, God, revealing Myself to the fore, teach you all the truth in detail.
You are calling this place the Jiba, the home of God, in Yamato;
But you do not know of its origin.
If you are told of this origin in full,
Great yearning will come over you, whoever you may be.
If you wish to hear and will come to Me,
I will tell you the truth that this place is the origin of any and everything.
When I, God, reveal Myself and teach you everything in detail, all people in the world will become cheerful.
As I hasten to save all of you equally,
I will set out to cheer up all the minds of the world.[191]

Christianity:

For this cause, we also, since the day we heard this, don't cease praying and making requests for you, that you may be filled with the knowledge of his will in all spiritual wisdom and understanding.[192]

---

[191] From *The Songs for the Teodorf Yorozuyo* (https://archive.org/details/mikagura-uta-the-songs-for-the-service./page/4/mode/2up).

[192] Colossians 1:9 (WEB).

135

Always rejoice. Pray without ceasing. In everything give thanks, for this is the will of God in Christ Jesus toward you.[193]

Not for these only do I pray, but for those also who will believe in me through their word, that they may all be one; even as you, Father, are in me, and I in you, that they also may be one in us; that the world may believe that you sent me. The glory which you have given me, I have given to them, that they may be one, even as we are one, I in them, and you in me, that they may be perfected into one, that the world may know that you sent me and loved them, even as you loved me.[194]

For in him we live, move, and have our being.' As some of your own poets have said, 'For we are also his offspring.'[195]

Philosophy:

PROP. XI. The first element, which constitutes the actual being of the human mind, is the idea of some particular thing actually existing.

Proof.—The essence of man is constituted by certain modes of the attributes of God, namely by the modes of thinking, of all which the idea is prior in nature, and, when the idea is given, the other modes (namely, those of which the idea is prior in nature) must be in the same individual (by the same Axiom). Therefore, an idea is the first element constituting the human mind. But not the idea of a non—existent thing, for then the idea itself cannot be said to exist; it must therefore be the idea of something actually existing. But not of an infinite thing. For an infinite thing must always necessarily exist; this would involve an absurdity. Therefore, the first element, which constitutes the actual being of the human mind, is the idea of something actually existing.

Corollary.—Hence it follows, that the human mind is part of the infinite intellect of God; thus when we say, that the human mind perceives

---

[193] 1st Thessalonians 5:16-18.

[194] John 17:20-23.

[195] Acts 17:28.

this or that, we make the assertion, that God has this or that idea, not in so far as he is infinite, but in so far as he is displayed through the nature of the human mind, or in so far as he constitutes the essence of the human mind; and when we say that God has this or that idea, not only in so far as he constitutes the essence of the human mind, but also in so far as he, simultaneously with the human mind, has the further idea of another thing, we assert that the human mind perceives a thing in part or inadequately.[196]

Stoicism[197]

Letter 41 – On the God within us. We do not need to uplift our hands towards heaven, or to beg the keeper of a temple to let us approach his idol's ear, as if in this way our prayers were more likely to be heard. God is near you, he is with you, he is within you. This is what I mean, Lucilius: a holy spirit indwells within us, one who marks our good and bad deeds, and is our guardian. As we treat this spirit, so are we treated by it. Indeed, no man can be good without the help of God.

If ever you have come upon a grove that is full of ancient trees which have grown to an unusual height, shutting out a view of the sky by a veil of pleached and intertwining branches, then the loftiness of the forest, the seclusion of the spot, and your marvel at the thick unbroken shade in the midst of the open spaces, will prove to you the presence of deity. Or if a cave, made by the deep crumbling of the rocks, holds up a mountain on its arch, a place not built with hands but hollowed out into such spaciousness by natural causes, your soul will be deeply moved by a certain intimation of the existence of God. ... Therefore, a greater part of it (soul) abides in that place from

---

[196] Excerpts from the writings of Baruch (Benedict) Spinoza (an excommunicated Jewish philosopher) "The Ethics" ("Ethica Ordine Geometrico Demonstrata") 1661-1675; translated from the Latin by R. H. M. Elwes
https://www.gutenberg.org/cache/epub/3800/pg3800-images.html

[197] Excerpts from Moral Letters to Lucilius by Seneca.
(https://en.wikisource.org/wiki/Moral_letters_to_Lucilius/Letter_41).

whence it came down to earth. Just as the rays of the sun do indeed touch the earth, but still abide at the source from which they are sent.

Hinduism: *That One, though motionless, is swifter than the mind. The senses can never overtake It, for It ever goes before. Though immovable, It travels faster than those who run. By It the all-pervading air sustains all living beings.[198]*

Zoroastrianism:

19. '(But) let each give ear to him who has conceived what is Right, an enlightened healer of the world, O Ahura, who will have power at will over the words of his tongue—so that they will be verified through Thy red Fire, O Mazda, in Thy good kingdom, at the New Dispensation (Judgment) by Thy two ministers.

20. 'Whosoever comes over to the righteous, for him hereafter will be spared the long duration of misery and darkness, the evil food and woeful words— such is that life to which, O ye wicked, your conscience through your own deeds will lead you.

21. 'May Ahura Mazda (then), out of His rich store grant unity with Weal and Immortality, with His Righteousness and Power,— (aye) the full enjoyment of the Good Mind, to him who is faithful to Him in word and deed. 22. 'Clear are these things to the wise as to one confident in mind; it is he that in word and deed promotes Righteousness with the Good Power, it is he, O Mazda, that will be to Thee a most profitable servant.[199]

---

[198] Isa Upanishad 4 (Paramananda).

[199] Zend-Avesta, Public domain "A Hymn of Zoroaster-Yasna 31" – by Willams Jackson, Abraham Valentine 1862-1937.

CHAPTER 5

THE DAWN OF ONENESS

INTRODUCTION

I remember that as a child I was able to hear a distinct internal voice that would speak to me from time to time. I just knew this as "the Voice." When I asked its name, the Voice told me not to worry about a name, just to know, "I am who was and is eternal and always will be." The Voice was a blissful presence. I asked my father about this Voice and he said to just be thankful to the Voice and to listen.

As I grew up, I noted that I was surrounded by people of various faiths, and I began to question the Voice about why there were so many faiths and conflicts between them. The Voice promised the answer would be revealed to me in time.

Soon enough, the Voice began to give me some simple words of truth, which I was to call: "Words on the Word to the World." These were insights from the words of various scriptures of religions speaking on the oneness of humanity and the oneness of God and oneness with God. I began to understand that it was the Voice that had spoken to people from time to time in history and given them a particular revelation. Sometimes the receiver or their followers created a new religion, and sometimes a religion simply made an adjustment in its course. This was all to benefit humanity.

Religious conflicts and peaceful resolutions can be understood in the microcosm of family life. If a father and mother have seven children and one is a doctor, one is an engineer, one is a thief, one is a murderer, one is a schoolteacher, one is a homemaker, and one is a drug addict, the parents still want the children to love one another, help one another, and rescue one another if needed. Never do the parents want the children to kill each other, especially over something that they said.

THE EARLY DAYS

In 1999, while I was living in Louisiana, Voice informed me in my prayers that I would meet someone who had the same calling as me. In August of that year I met Dawn, a physician for whom I became a business consultant. I provided business consultation for her medical practice, and with education and patience, her business turned around. It became evident during our conversations and prayers that we both had the same calling. Alongside promoting oneness, we felt called to work with orphanages and feed the hungry. The Voice told Dawn and me, in our separate prayers, that we were to be married to learn more for ourselves about oneness and to be an example of oneness, so we married in 2003 in a unique Oneness of God ceremony incorporating many wedding rituals practiced by people of various faiths and cultures.

My wife, Dawn, and I formed a foundation to promote oneness. Our plans to accomplish this mission included arranging gatherings of different religions in different countries to share and mutually exchange the positives and common elements of each religion, thus enabling the people to see, on their own, the importance of each one to God. In this process, through like-minded individuals, this oneness would spread with an attitude of respect instead of condemnation, and in such a manner that these individuals would not compromise their own ongoing charitable works. We also initiated tangible works of service to the downtrodden, outcast, hungry, and orphaned. We are continuing our efforts to reach national leaders, and with their concurrence and cooperation in promoting this oneness, it will continue to spread.

Our early works included oneness home meetings. We invited friends from various religions to come and learn from one another's faith. These meetings were followed by brief silent worship and prayerful meditation together, and then time to socialize. We also conducted peace forums, which were public meetings in auditoriums, based on the same format as the home meetings. They began with a panel of people from different religions each offering a brief summary of their faith, followed by an opportunity for questions and answers (no debating—just seeking clarity and knowledge) and then brief simultaneous silent meditative prayer and worship, followed by socializing. Most meetings lasted about an hour. The home meetings and public peace forums were always friendly and well received. It was understood that each person would be taken seriously and would be allowed to speak without interruption within a specified time frame, and everyone in the space would respect their beliefs and experiences as unique and equally valid.

The purpose of these gatherings is to simply learn about each other's spiritual practice. We let go of the need to resolve disagreements, which are present in everybody's family anyway. This was our way of opening a door and letting light stream into a dark place, so to speak. Each person took from this experience new thoughts. In addition, they had a new reference point: having had the experience of worshipping the one God in oneness, they could no longer say it couldn't be done. In our travels overseas, we continued this pattern of peace forums and home meetings.

During the silent worship and prayerful meditation portions of our meetings and forums, I saw attendees from all these different religions lay down every weapon—including their own opinions—in order to engage this higher realm. This oneness worship is key. That is the level of submission that is required to accomplish something higher than each individual could on their own. Our goal and desire is not one world religion, as you can see, but all religions in oneness. Some in our meetings resisted this practice at first, but when they entered into it, they found the fruit of it was peace, in themselves and the group. In other words, one organism, so to speak, is created in a oneness meeting: the entanglement of each individual enfolded within One God. If you are from Zimbabwe, for example, you might call this 'ubuntu' (*I am because you are*). If you are a physicist, you could call this 'quantum entanglement.' I see Oneness as a matter of being and not in doing; "doing" flows out of "being," not the other way around.

I could see in my mind and my prayers that the oneness home meetings could be used to bring societies, cultures, and religions together in a safe environment. Here, they could learn from one another how to reframe their own spirituality and how to transform themselves, their families, and their culture and society to living as one with peace and joy, in love—and all without being expected to change their religion.

When such an occasion is shared, then all reap the oneness experience simultaneously. This has an elevated energy of its own, propelling joy even higher. I have seen this happen and it is a transforming experience. It is the juice that flows whenever oneness is practiced.

The participants then begin to say, "I am a_____ (fill in the blank with your own religion or use such terms as atheist, irreligious, etc.) who practices Oneness."

My observations in life and in prayer are that this oneness starts in the individual first. As a person practices oneness within themselves—spending time in prayer and meditation, experiencing greater and greater peace, implementing the twelve principles of oneness, and releasing the love within their own life—then it can spread to small societal groups and continue to flow through society. This love from spending time with the Voice has changed me forever. This has been the pattern of my personal journey to oneness—from pleasure to pain, and now, Peace.

What we have been able to accomplish through our foundation is only the tip of the iceberg—in my prayers and spiritual encounters, I have seen that so much more can be done for this calling. We began to learn the basics of how to build infrastructure for oneness, but we also learned that timing is in the hands of the Voice. All things must be done from the position of resting in the Divine, for this reveals the evidence of true faith. We learned patience in this resting, and it still serves us well. Dawn and I feel we have been longing for oneness (or "ekatva," meaning oneness in Sanskrit) for a very long time. We knew these early successes were to establish our own understanding of strategy and the value of building a foundation within ourselves. We know the fruit of this "ekatva" will come later, even after we have left this earth.

ONENESS WITH ALL, IN ALL, AND FOR ETERNITY

Oneness is not the same as co-existence or tolerance, because both of these concepts still keep us apart. We may treat one another with mutual irrelevance, but this resembles apathy more than oneness. Oneness is not sameness.

In all this time we have been dedicating our lives to oneness, we have seen that the appreciation and implementation of the Twelve Principles of Oneness by the people who attended these meetings had a powerful effect on promoting oneness in their own lives. This was because they all could visualize the same thing, even if from their own perspective. It is like a group of people watching a sunrise together— they are all gazing at the same sun rising and sharing in this moment of awe and beauty, yet they each see it from their own angle. Similarly, in our meetings, though each person's experience was individual and unique, what they were all seeing was the same: the birth of oneness in themselves and the group.

If you look at the footprint of God in every religion and find yourself condemning someone else's God, you may have accidentally condemned your own God. It is important to repent, seek forgiveness, and seek the right way through your prayer and meditation. Understand the forgiving power and nature of God and start worshipping in oneness with love for the One God so that you can have peace and joy from now through eternity. Doesn't God want the members of all religions to experience living in peace with love and joy, just like any parent would want their own children to do? This is of the utmost priority for the betterment of society in the world today.

I encourage you to simply and quietly open your mind and your spirit to the Voice, to love, to wisdom, and ask this Voice to speak so you can hear. Simply making an effort daily for ten minutes over the course of a month will be well worth the investment.

Every day between the hours of 6:00 a.m. and 7:00 a.m., and again between 6:00 p.m. and 7:00 p.m. (USA Pacific Time), my wife and I spend time in prayer and meditation specifically for oneness. Please join us for this simultaneous global oneness prayer time, if only for five to ten minutes during one of these time slots, as this is one of the most fruitful things we can do to promote peace throughout the world.

This book is the essence of what I have heard from the Voice and seen in my earthly and heavenly walks with the Voice. I have seen in my visions that oneness will continue to spread and the joy it promotes will even bless the land. The Voice also informed me in a sweet way that I will not be on this earth when this movement begins to accelerate. If you are reading this book, I have prayed for you.

DO YOU HAVE THIS CALLING?

The time to move forward is now, as the hunger for oneness is growing worldwide. In our travels we hear again and again of this hunger. Many feel the birth pangs of a notable universal spiritual movement, and they are saying things like, "Something is afoot!" Oneness was, is, and always will be a reality in the heart of the Ultimate Truth, the True One God, the Voice.

CHAPTER 6

TESTIMONIES

The following are the words of a few people from different parts of the world. These people were of diverse ages, levels of education, socio-economic backgrounds, professions, faiths and notoriety. These quotes were taken from conversations I had with them (some of them individually and others in small groups) in which I was able to share the ideas that form this book.

An Atheist Lt. Colonel:

What I have heard from you on the subject of Oneness has made me change my outlook on what I believed in so far. The subtle manner in which you answered my questions—asking me as a first step to substitute the words "Science," "Self-intellect," "A power like air I cannot see but can feel and experience," "Nobility," or "Whatever suits me" for the word God; and to substitute the words "Think," "Contemplate quietly," or "Whatever suits me" for the word "Pray"—touched me and helped me. I experienced a peace I never had in my entire life.

A Famous Bollywood Movie Actor:

I consider myself neither an atheist nor a theist but a realist. On my own, I never went to a church, a temple, a mosque or any worship place, nor prayed at home anytime. I have only ever been to mosques, churches, temples and worship places to worship as part of my role as a movie actor. But I liked what I heard on Oneness from you and therefore I have agreed to take part in initiating Oneness propagation. My Best Wishes to you and please move on with your efforts.

An Agnostic Couple:

We as agnostics don't know whether there is a God or not. If there is a God, everything is God. We did not like some people condemning us, calling us sinners, idolaters. No one likes to listen to someone who starts with a criticism even on non-spiritual matters. Why would anyone listen to someone who speaks words of condemnation on such important matters like my faith, belief, and spirituality? What I have heard from you on Oneness, the content and the process are very pleasing, and it is what most in the present-day world need to hear to advance and transform.

A Scholar and Professor of Islamic Studies:

It is a fact that there has been so much bloodshed using the name of God and religion, perhaps more than any other cause in human history so far. As a Muslim, I have intensively studied Islam and been teaching Islamic studies for years. I can tell you that what I have heard from you today are not your words. They are from Allah. How can any faith or religion refuse what you have shared? What you shared does not negate the core of any religion. It helps every faith and religion in their understanding of Allah and that they have limited themselves to what they already know. It helps everyone to be able to share their faith with and learn from others. Like Muhammed (peace be upon his name) was asked to move on in propagating what God gave him, regardless of people accepting it or not, you should move forward propagating what you shared with me today. If you do not, you are disobeying God and wasting what God gave you to do. You may not be an influential person for the world to accept it easily. One day, humanity will realize the value of it and it will be a seed now and become a main instrument and vehicle in bringing an end to the bloodshed using the name of God and religion. Everyone should welcome what you have to share.

A Catholic Priest:

What I heard from you about Oneness is from God. The words are not yours. You are chosen by God to give this message. I have wondered often why different faiths and religions have been groping in darkness like the four blind men touching an elephant and each describing the elephant as only the part they touched, felt, and experienced. Oneness is like giving the total perspective of the elephant. God has spoken to different faiths in different ways, but through you, God has shown us in the simplest possible form how we should practice living in our daily walks of life. God bless you in your propagating what He gave you. I feel honored to say these words and give you my blessings.

A Protestant Christian Pastor and His Wife:

We have been in the ministry of preaching, teaching and mission works, doing the Lord's work for years. What we heard from you on ONENESS and what God is doing through you is profound. It gave us goose bumps as we were listening to you. This is what the world needs now. We will keep you in our prayers and seek the Lord to guide us on our role in this work of His.

A Christian Evangelist from Argentina:

This is profound and very much needed for world peace; this is what every religion, theologian, and common man needs to hear, practice and propagate. Your propagating it is not going to be an easy task. It will be a lonely walk for a long time. God bless you and be with you.

A Christian Evangelist from USA

You have an apostolic calling.

A Buddhist Monk:

You have received wisdom that is needed for the present-day world to hear, much like Buddha received wisdom that was needed for his time. I have never heard something like this so far. It is amazing. Your selfless effort of sharing and propagating this without looking for any personal reward are commendable. Carry on your work.

A Confucianism Practitioner:

What I heard from you is simple, practical, non-controversial and necessary—like the teachings of Confucius. Good luck.

A Hindu Scholar (and Business Magnate) and His Wife:

We do not know and cannot say what other religious books and the views of scholars and theologians might be on this. The entire humanity needs to hear this. It needs a lot of resources to do the work of propagating. God will give you the people, resources, and everything. We will do our part not only in words but through actions within our power. Paul Harris started the Rotary Club with just a few friends and few resources, and it is now international without any religious affiliation. This is what is great about the idea of Oneness you shared. It is not a religion and yet should be acceptable to every religion and human being. Oneness will reach much greater heights and acceptance one day. Who knows, even Rotary may associate with this effort one day.

A Shinto Practitioner:

The simplicity and adaptability of Oneness and your words on preserving nature touched me. I will think more about it and see if there is any reason why I should not adopt it and see what transformation takes place in me through this as days go by.

A Taoist Practitioner:

I am totally attracted. It does not ask me to give up what I believe in or what I am doing; it offers a gradual transformation in my heart through seeing and learning good in everyone's ways, and enabling others to see the good in my ways through setting an example. That is what it is advocating—not anything that is offensive or controversial. I will start putting it into practice a little at a time before I share with others.

A Brahma Kumari Samaj Devotee Family:

Our entire family is devoted and dedicated to the practice of Brahma Kumari Samaj. We do not have to give up anything. We are in agreement with Oneness in its entirety. We are committed to helping propagate Oneness.

A Jain Physician:

It is said greatness lies in simplicity. What a great and simple way I have heard today, to live a noble life and for humanity to live in peace and joy, integrating the good of all faiths.

A Sikh Business Executive:

I am a Sikh bearing the name Singh. One of the main thrusts of my faith is to be a learner (meaning of the word Sikh) and Singh means a lion (king of animals), and therefore to be a leader and like a lion in learning is very foundational and fundamental to what I believe in. Oneness falls in line with what our gurus (masters) and our book (Guru Granth Sahib) have taught us.

A Jewish Secretary:

This is what I needed to hear to live my life; there are so many confusing and contradicting messages given by theologians, it is hard to understand theology or how to have a deeper life in God. What a wonderful blessing it is for me today in what I heard. This simple Oneness helps me to have inner peace and know how gracious God has been in giving me this opportunity to hear what I heard today. It is said Jesus Christ was a Jew but rejected by Jews. I hope the same does not happen to this simple man propagating Oneness. I only hope that every religion and faith would view this Oneness as complementary and supplemental to their faith.

A Drug Addict:

This is the first time in my life I have heard about God in such a simple way. For me, it was too good and too simple to believe. I had always experienced people condemning me and making me feel I was doomed anyway, that I would be going to hell, so why bother changing? Why not go on with rest of my life the way I was? What I heard today was simple. It showed me I have worth and gave me more respect for myself and love of God than I have ever heard. Regardless of what others said in the past and what anyone might say in the future, I will be unshaken. I will cure myself, be a good person, and become a model for my near and dear to look to through the love I show. I will start spending time in praying regularly. I will only take the positives of what I hear, ignore all other stuff I hear from others, and start studying and learning about God as much as I can. I will spend my time prayerfully asking God to forgive me and help me resist daily temptations and negative influences. I will spend my time with family and the close ones sharing with them Oneness and righteousness. If everyone gets an opportunity to hear what I heard today, there will be more God-loving people and less of the sorts of things I did. God help you in giving this Oneness message to humanity.

A Female Bi-sexual Student:

It started as fun, then it became a habit. Right or wrong, I do not know. I don't know why I felt like sharing about myself with you, a total stranger I sat next to in the airplane; why I asked you what you think about gays, lesbians and bisexuals, God, gay bishops being accepted in the world even while homosexuals are still being condemned, and so on. The caring and positive words you said to me, and the respect, appreciation, and admiration you expressed for the passive, compassionate, and caring nature of people like me, took me by surprise—it was contrary to what I have been bombarded with. You spoke not one word of condemnation. You answered every question not with theology but with simplicity, and humorous examples for me to understand God and the love of God and the forgiveness of God. What you told me of my worth to God, and what God means, how I can start understanding God, and the twelve principles of Oneness for me to begin to walk in a godly way in all areas of my life was simple. It was like a learning experience that would need a lifetime to understand, being given on a silver platter. Your words were interesting, and the time flew by faster than the airplane. I promise to change and share with my close friends and stay in touch with you.

A Lap Dancer:

You remember the day I and my friends watched you doing the Cha Cha dance at the ballroom dance exhibition on the dance floor? My friends and I had just come out for a girls' night out. When I asked you for a dance and told you that I and my friends were lap dancers, you did not make gestures like some men would do. I don't know why, but we felt like asking you about God; we shared our frustrations in life and outlook and how we feel we are stuck, and then asked if there was a way some of us (who wanted to turn to better and more godly ways of living) can know about God and begin to lead our lives in a godly way. We know that life as lap dancers is not the best way to live. It was going to be a short-term thing of a few months or a few years of our youth. What you shared then touched all of us.

We did not know it would be that easy and practical and simple to understand and adopt. One of my friends told you that she was a Muslim and asked about Muhammad's ascension to Heaven and Holy War and Islam. The profound respect you showed for Islam and what you shared about your godly experience at the Dubai airport touched her. Another friend of mine was a Christian and asked you, "The Bible says that after crucifixion Jesus Christ was to be in the tomb for three days and three nights before resurrection. But, wasn't it only three days and two nights He was in the tomb? Isn't the Bible wrong?" Your explanation of the Jewish way of counting day and night appealed to her so much, she said that it was the simplest and most accurate answer she ever heard, and she was convinced that the Bible was not wrong, and nobody else had ever given her a straight answer whenever she had asked.

What you told us of God's ways, love and forgiveness, putting the past behind and moving forward, and how to walk in godly ways in all walks of life, as well as the write-up on the Twelve Principles of Oneness you gave us, transformed three of the five of us that were there that day. One is now married and has a child, one is engaged, and I have a boyfriend who smiles at me whenever I talk about meeting you and what you told us about God and the godly way of living. We both are trying our best to live that way. Sometimes it appears difficult but praying and putting in an effort has been much better than not trying at all and gives us peace in our mind and hearts. You go and touch many lives with the message God gave you. Thank God we met you.

An Endowment Advisor to a Large Nation:

I have studied various religions and faiths. Many a saint and sage in history started Oneness. God called them to do so. This is not the first time. But they turned to themselves to start their own faiths, process of rituals, and so on. Oneness never took off. What I heard from you is from God. I am delighted that you are not calling it a new religion but bringing all together as one and of the one God. That is what the world needs now. Stay on with it and do your work and it will succeed.

A Congressman in Washington:

What I heard from you is profound. It is required in the world very much today more than ever. It may take a much longer process and time to be accepted and adopted in rich nations and countries. Immediate need and acceptance are more likely at present in countries like Nigeria and Ghana. I will write to the presidents of these two nations I know well, introducing you. Let us see how they respond. I will look into all possible ways I can help you serve this selfless purpose and calling of God.

A Retired UN Advisor to Europe:

I served as UN Advisor to a few European countries for some time. Later, I came to know about Oneness from someone—it is amazing to me. So I came to meet you to know more detail. Now, what I heard from you has enhanced it. This oneness is what the world needs. Every possible support for this to reach every nook and corner of the earth should be given. At a time when it is controversial to display the Ten Commandments because they are from only one particular religion, the Twelve Principles of Oneness can have an impact because they are of no one religion. They are non-controversial, should be acceptable to all, and are practical for day-to-day life in all walks of life. Maybe God has a reason why I did not know of this while I was working in my capacity as UN Advisor. Even then it would have taken time to be endorsed by the UN as the process is genuinely challenging for the right reasons, but it may take much longer now. But at least something can be done, and I will do what I can, because the Twelve Principles of Oneness are as much as or more deserving than anything endorsed by the UN in the past. I am glad I met you and talked to you and heard from you directly. It has been a blessing to me. God bless you and thank you.

A Family in India:

After knowing about the time you spent fasting and praying, we asked you to heal our daughter who was suffering from a birth defect for almost thirty years. You said you were not a healer but, even if you were ill, you would ask God in prayers for God's will to be done—and God would heal if that be God's will. You prayed for her, for God's will to be done, and you asked us to daily pray for her in faith. You asked your friends to pray for her too. We started diligently implementing the Twelve Principles of Oneness. A yearlong prayer per your guidelines asking God in faith to do God's will for her miraculously helped and she is now completely cured. Thank you.

In fact, it was these words from this family that prompted me to begin fulfilling my responsibility to write and present this book. Recognition for me or the above individuals has not been our motto; any recognition should be for those who accept Oneness, adopt it, and transform in their thoughts, words and actions. Therefore, though one day the names of the above or mine are likely to be known, please do not concentrate on that aspect as we have decided to stay away from seeking personal recognition. Therefore, their names are not given, and my name was not given until now. Help us to stay away from personal recognition. Consider for yourself what you read, set aside or contemplate what you cannot readily accept, and put into practice what you can. If you can, propagate these principles individually, or if you want to help us do so, please write to us.

CHAPTER 7

SIMPLE WORDS OF TRUTH IN A NUTSHELL

In the present-day world, people are much busier than ever before. It is not going to get any better as far as availability of time is concerned. While the priorities from individual to individual are different, it seems like taking time for the spiritual aspect of life, praying, and worship is not a priority for most people, at least not as much as is needed.

Therefore, let me give a short synopsis of the contents of this book so far, which will provide a good foundation for understanding the Twelve Principles of Oneness. The contents of different chapters provide answers to most questions that might arise as well as necessary elaborations on some points. However, though the following simple recap may look elementary, it should help in understanding the most important points.

People can be classified into three major groups: Atheists, Agnostics, and Believers. The primary causes of bloodshed for religious reasons are: the divisions among the believers; a self-centered desire for power and control; and wanting everyone else to accept, convert to and practice a particular faith.

One who does not believe in God or is not sure if there is a God at all may consider, as a first step, substituting another word for the term "God," such as "Nobility," "Truth," "Love," "Wisdom" or "Common Values and Principles with Which All of Humanity Can Live" (regardless of the location, culture and local laws different people live by). At the same time, they should remain open-minded, waiting to see what transformation takes place within themselves.

Believers of all religions have to know that God has manifested at different times in different ways (directly or through chosen individuals) to eradicate wickedness, reestablish righteousness, and save the righteous according to God's timing and will. Those who claim their faith is the only faith and the only way to God, and who try to impose their own faith on others, need to deeply consider the following essential points:

If your faith is the only way, what about the rest of humanity that was there for ages before your faith came into existence?

God is selfless love. Whatever truth, good thoughts, good words, and good actions there are in other faiths are all from God.

No one has ever known God fully, as God has only revealed himself as much as was required depending upon the context. Therefore, unless you know God in others' ways, you have not known your own God completely.

By the same token, if you criticize the God of others, you are criticizing your own God. It is only the traditions, beliefs, interpretations, superstitions, rituals, practices and such that vary among faiths. As long as these variations do not involve evil or harm to others, do not attach importance to these variations.

Everyone must realize that the means to visualize and experience God vary wildly from one person to another, depending upon one's mental framework. Therefore, everyone should remain open-minded and realize that experiencing God beyond any physical shape or earthly object is vital for the fulfillment of life. It is a gradual process that takes time, and it is much more important than insisting that others formally convert to a particular faith or philosophy (which often leads to nothing more than formal conversion and continued groping in darkness even after conversion).

Every moment of a human being's life—and every thought, word, and action—falls into one or more of these seven categories:

Spirituality, Family, Finance, Health, Entertainment (activities for fun, relaxation, rejuvenation), Building a Personal Relationship with someone, and Societal Service. Within these domains, there are three ways one might lead a daily life: the Godly way (selfless love), the human way (self-centered), and the evil way (harming others).

Human beings usually live in some combination of all three ways in different parts of their life: the Godly way in some areas of life, the selfish way in others, and the evil way in still others. Sometimes in one domain of life they live in a Godly way and at other times in the very same domain they behave in a selfish or evil way, depending upon the circumstances, situations and temptations. What God wants us to do is live in a Godly way in all areas of our life all the time. This is what human beings need to know now: how to live in a Godly way in all areas of life.

The Twelve Principles of Oneness outline how to do this. These Twelve Principles, received during fasting and praying, were given to me to share with the world. They are the principles common to every faith which would be acceptable to all faiths, regardless of their outward appearance, and to all people, regardless of their lifestyles.

CHAPTER 8

Eternal Voice and Wisdom

Dear Reader,

If this book helps you in any manner, enabling you to lead a better life with selfless, godly love for yourself, others and God, rejoice and thank whoever prompted you to read this book. And, if you can, also thank God (the Truth, Gracious Love, the Right Way, the Righteous Way, the Light that removes darkness in our hearts, All the Noblest Attributes in One). Do this, and we will feel you helped us fulfill the purpose of our lives. I thank you in advance for that.

Whatever elements of this book appeared confusing or questionable or not acceptable to you, please simply set them aside. The same elements may have been very much admired, accepted, and adopted by someone else. Therefore, as the days go by and as you ponder the ideas in this book, even those aspects you initially set aside may become meaningful, acceptable and even adoptable to you. Until then, please adopt only whatever was fresh and resonant for you.

We want to reiterate that "Oneness" is not a new religion. We don't need another religion. Oneness is also not about adopting every aspect of every belief system, nor is it religious syncretism. You may have heard people use the idea of "oneness" in other ways. But the way we are speaking about Oneness here is different. Here, we are bringing forward into focus those core aspects of religious faith that are acceptable and important to most systems of spiritual belief, thereby allowing us to see how united we actually already are, even with all our differences. Understanding the Oneness that pervades all spiritual faiths can help us live without bloodshed caused in the name of God; it can help us live with mutual respect, in peace and joy, with godly love in all walks of life; it can help us serve those in need with selfless love; finally, it can help us adore and worship the One God (Truth) wholeheartedly.

We request that you not use, nor trust anyone who uses Oneness or the name of Oneness or the contents of this book for personal, corporate, or institutional recognitions, rewards, societal status, or financial or political gains. By respecting those who diligently adopt and propagate Oneness, you will certainly be an encouragement and inspiration to others; it will be a blessing to you, for you have eternity in your heart.

If you find that what you gained from this book is useful, and you'd like to help others learn about it, we invite you to become a Oneness admirer, practitioner, propagator, torch bearer or volunteer. Join hands with other individuals, institutions or their chapters that propagate Oneness so it may reach and be adopted by all. Please let us know if you are not sure about how to help, as we can offer guidance. Contact us by checking out our website at www.onenessmission.world

With wholehearted gratitude, Ramanjaneyulu (Rom) Tanguturi and Dawn Knight Tanguturi (Eagle Vision Foundation co-founders).

***

When in deep prayer recently, I was caught up into the atmosphere above earth and Voice gave me a strong bow and then a flaming torch arrow of love, and together we shot it from the Heavenly realm to earth and we watched as the flame of love passed from one heart to the next, many times over. I saw our prayer answered right before my eyes, and the words of love spoken to me from Voice at that time cannot be uttered, for they are too sweet.

In Gratitude,
Papa Ram
September 2023

ABOUT THE AUTHOR

Ramanjaneyulu (Rom) Tanguturi was an engineer and business and management consultant, having received his MBA from the Indian Institute of Management in Ahmedebad, India.

From the time he was ten years old, he could hear the internal audible Voice of God and began asking this Voice why there were so many religions and so much conflict and bloodshed resulting from the misuse of religion and the name of God. The Voice told him he would learn about that as he grew up. Later, Ram went on a downward spiral in his life that transformed who he thought he was and what his life was for. He described feeling as though he had gone from "something" to nothing.

He began to hear the Voice again, and the Voice led him all over the world to explore his lifelong questions. After an extensive period of fasting and prayer, the Voice gave him twelve principles for living in Oneness that do not conflict with any religion's core principles. How we can apply these so that the whole world can live in peace and joy, serving humanity and worshipping God in oneness, became Ram's own journey. Ram knew he had then become something from nothing, and the Voice became everything.

In 2003 Ram married Dawn Knight in Louisiana. They formed Eagle Vision Foundation for the purpose of promoting Peace and Joy through Oneness of Humanity with the One God and Worshipping in Oneness with Love (the mission statement). Their foundation has conducted Oneness home meetings and public peace forums in India,

Cambodia, Nigeria, the USA, Vietnam, and Panama, while also supporting orphanages, building water projects for schools, and building homes for families of the victims of the 2004 Indian Ocean Tsunami.

Ram had been writing on his journey to Oneness for many years, and he completed his book while in Panama in June 2023. The Voice called Ram Home in October of 2023, and Dawn continues the work of publishing his books. It was Ram's passion to help the underprivileged as guided by the Voice. Ram lived to do the will of the Voice and completed his calling and mission. Ram lived to be One with God.

Papa Ram (Ramanjaneyulu (Rom) Tanguturi), 1942-2023

APPENDIX

-Twelve Principles of Oneness™

-Oneness Prayer and Meditations

-An Atheist's Prayer (a.k.a. the Wisdom Prayer)

-More Resources

-Photos from my journey

-List of Twelve Groups of religions discussed in Chapter 2 the Voice Through the Ages

-List of "Prayers and Passages" from Chapter 3 - Spirit Words: the Voice Through the Hearts of People

-Mission Statement (of this book, of our foundation and of my life)

-An Exhortation from Papa

APPENDIX A

TWELVE PRINCIPLES OF ONENESS™

1. **Love, worship and honor God** with praise, obedience, sacrifice, humility, and seeking forgiveness. Place God first in every thought, word, and action.

2. **God is almighty, present all over, all knowing and most gracious.** Experiencing God beyond any physical shape or earthly object is vital. Do not use God's name for selfish or unrighteous purposes.

3. **Love and honor parents** with care all their lives, in obedience and respect.

4. **Love and honor, with respect and humility, the ones who teach you righteousness** and what they teach you.

5. **Love your family** with humility, time and cheer—taking care of them, encouraging them to lead a closer walk with God, and setting an example.

6. **Love your neighbors**, forgiving their wrongdoings and showing greater care for your neighbors' possessions and life than you would for your own.

7. **Love the poor, sick, old, weak, handicapped, orphans, widows, lonely, abused, outcasts and downtrodden** with compassion—giving them what they need as much as you can.

8. **Stay away from envy, greed, self-centered pride, anger, gluttony, lust (unrighteous desire), sloth (laziness) and unrighteous attachments**—to refrain from the temptation of evil.

9. **Respect and learn good in others' ways and beliefs** enabling them to learn good from your faith and works more than from your words.

10. **Maintain your body with care**, as the soul given by God lives in it, and **preserve and respect nature and all the creation of God**, selectively utilizing the resources for righteous purposes.

11. **Spend one day a week in worship**, spiritual enrichment, enhancement of family togetherness and physical rest, meeting only the needs you must and fasting as led in your prayers.

12. **Pray without ceasing** for oneness, peace, and joy for all, asking God to help you do God's will, to reach God, the Ultimate, and to attain Oneness with God.

*****

APPENDIX B

ONENESS PRAYER AND MEDITATIONS

(May be addressed to "True One God, Divine Consciousness, Ultimate Truth or your own personal name for the One Ultimate Reality)

I am grateful for the experience of growing in love as I humbly gaze at the expansive universe in which I dwell and which dwells in me. I will never fully comprehend this amazing world that I look to for wisdom, love and truth.

I will examine myself for harmful tendencies or actions and seek forgiveness and mercy from all I have harmed. In return, I extend the same forgiveness and mercy, as I want to live a life without harming others physically, emotionally or financially—a life of oneness and peace with all others.

I am grateful for the provisions needed for life, the unmerited favor I enjoy, and the noble role models set before me as I work towards being an example of honor, respect and kindness to those near and dear to me as well as the world around me.

I will keep an open mind and open heart towards love and truth in all realms and I will live a life in which truth and love prevail, walking in humility in this universe, with which I am one.

Thank you, thank you, thank you!
Ramanjaneyulu (Rom) Tanguturi

This may be read or prayed in its entirety as a single prayer or each meditation can be individually and deeply contemplated during a meditation session.

APPENDIX C

AN ATHEIST'S PRAYER
(A.K.A. THE WISDOM PRAYER)

Wisdom stands before me.
I can walk with wisdom for my journey.
I will let wisdom be my teacher and virtue be my guide as I walk down
the path of love.

I will seek to learn from the wisdom of others, and I will let my life be a
teacher of wisdom and respect.

I will always seek to respect others and learn from them while being an
example of the wisdom I have learned during this life, paid for with
time.

I will treat others as I like to be treated and I will train my children in
this way. I will care for my family, and I will be grateful for their love
and care for me.

I will not harm anyone physically, emotionally or financially.
I will help the needy when I can, and I am grateful for the resources
that I have to do so.

I will take care of the earth, my home, and respect its gifts and humbly
gaze at its beauty.

I am quantum entangled with all in the universe, and I choose to live
with respect for nature which has been my home in this life. I will
meditate on these good things.

I am grateful for the time I had to learn and live, and I freely give to others my knowledge and my love.

Ramanjaneyulu (Rom) Tanguturi

The above is suitable for reading at any type of significant event such as a wedding, funeral, or any type of solemn occasion, especially when sacred language is desired without assigning religion. The poem can be read by one person or in an alternating responsive way by the audience.

Appendix D

More Resources

All scriptures and writings are from public domain sources unless otherwise indicated.

Confucianism: https://www.gutenberg.org/cache/epub/3330/pg3330-images.html

Zoroastrianism, Islam: https://www.gutenberg.org/files/12894/12894-h/12894-h.htm

Islam: https://www.gutenberg.org/cache/epub/16955/pg16955-images.html

Christianity: https://ebible.org/engwmb/index.htm

Judaism: https://archive.org/details/1917JPSTanakhInHebrewAndEnglish/mode/2up

Hinduism: https://www.gutenberg.org/files/2388/2388-h/2388-h.htm https://archive.org/details/srimad-bhagavatam-by-kamala-subramaniam/page/n3/mode/2up and

https://www.gutenberg.org/files/39442/39442-h/39442-h.html#the-twelfth-skandha and

https://www.gutenberg.org/cache/epub/3283/pg3283.html

Tenrikyo: https://archive.org/details/mikagura-uta-the-songs-for-the-service./page/4/mode/2up

Buddhism: https://www.gutenberg.org/files/30216/30216-h/30216-h.htm#chap04 and

https://archive.org/details/heartprajna/page/n1/mode/2up

https://www.gutenberg.org/files/64623/64623-h/64623-h.htm

https://www.gutenberg.org/cache/epub/2017/pg2017-images.html#link2HCH0020

Sikhism: https://archive.org/details/SriGuruGranthSahibJi-InGurmukhiRomanisedEnglish/page/n785/mode/2up

Jainism: https://archive.org/details/tattvarthbook10webf/page/n13/mode/2up

Shintoism: https://archive.org/details/mythslegendsofja00davi

Taoism: https://www.gutenberg.org/cache/epub/216/pg216-images.html

Bahá'í Faith: https://Bahá'í.org and https://bahai-library.com/writings/bahaullah/aqdas/aqdas.html

Indigenous spirituality: https://sacred-texts.com/afr/indes.htm
And https://sacred-texts.com/nam/index.htm

APPENDIX E

PHOTOS FROM MY JOURNEY TO ONENESS

On a Prayer retreat in Louisiana, USA.

Teaching at a Yoga Teacher training course in the Dalles, Oregon, USA.
Published with permission from Pure Yoga Teacher Training, the Dalles, Oregon.

I completed the Portland Marathon in 2016. I took up running after my 70th birthday, when my wife gave me running shoes and a book about running when you are older. I discovered I could extend my contemplative prayer and meditation while running.

I am in my late teens here, on the horse with my young relative on the way to a family event celebrating the young child's education milestone in India.

APPENDIX F

LIST OF TWELVE GROUPS OF RELIGIONS DISCUSSED IN CHAPTER 2 THE VOICE THROUGH THE AGES

-Indigenous Spirituality

-Judaism

-Christianity

-Islam

-Bahai Faith

-Zoroastrianism

-Jainism

-Hinduism

-Sikhism

-Buddhism

-Chinese Traditions and Faiths

    -Taoism

    -Confucianism

-Japanese Traditions and Faiths

    -Shintoism

    -Tenrikyo

Appendix G

List of "Prayers and Passages" from Chapter 3 - Spirit Words: the Voice Through the Hearts of People

Common Prayers

1. - Breath Prayer examples
2. - My Morning Prayer Example

Model Prayers and Meditations from Various Religions

1. Indigenous People's Prayer for Loss of a Loved One
2. On the Goal of Meditation – Islamic Sufism
3. Prayer for Wisdom and an Honorable Posterity – Islamic prayer
4. On the Importance of Truth in Prayer – Sikhism
5. Model Prayer for Your Unique Destiny and Purpose – Christian
6. Prayer for Intimacy with God and Intercession for Others – Christian
7. Prayer to Dedicate My Life to Oneness
8. Daily Prayer Seeking the Presence of God
9. Disciple's Prayer (a.k.a. the "Lord's Prayer") – Christianity (Bible, Matthew Chapter 6)
10. Mantra from Rig Veda – Hinduism
11. Mantra from Tibetan Buddhism
12. Buddhist Prayer and Psalm
13. Prayer for Forgiveness and Redemption
14. An Atheist's Prayer – aka the Wisdom Prayer
15. Moses' Blessing Prayer – Jewish Scriptures
16. Oneness Prayer and Meditations

A. Gratitude

B. Self-examination

C. Exhortation

D. Humility and Acknowledgment

Passages from Scriptures, Poetry and Songs of Various Religions, Traditions, Faiths and Philosophies

1. Excerpts from the Japji – III Sikh Scriptures
2. The Hope of a Man of Worth – Excerpts from Proverbs 31 -from the Jewish Tanakh
3. Knowing Your Prayer Will Be Heard – from Jewish scriptures
4. Tenrikyo Literature
    Song V

5 - Quotes from the Analects of Confucius
    Book 1
    Book 2
    Book 3
    Book 4
    Book 5

6 - The Great Supreme – Taoist Literature

7 - Stoicism – The Meditations of the Emperor Marcus Aurelius Antoninus

8 - On the Benefits of Oneness of Humanity from the Islamic Scriptures – the Quran

9 - Buddhist Psalm of Paradise

10 - On Not Worrying and Laying Up Treasures in Heaven – Christian Scriptures - Luke 12

11 - Heaven and Earth Endure, Tao Te Ching – Taoism Chapter 7

12 - The Seed Bestowed on Them by the Gods of Heaven - Shintoism (Description from Oral Renderings)

13 - Bhagavad Gita (the Song of God) – Hindu Scriptures Chapter XII

MISSION STATEMENT

**To Promote and Bring
Peace and Joy
through Oneness of Humanity
with the One God and
Worshipping in Oneness
with Love**

May You Cherish, Follow, Share and Pass the Wisdom on to Your Near and Dear and Generations to Come~

With Abundant and Merciful Love,
PAPA

www.ingramcontent.com/pod-product-compliance
Lightning Source LLC
Chambersburg PA
CBHW031317120626
46554CB00001BA/451